SPECTRUM

Test Prep

Grade 4

SPECTRUM

Columbus, Ohio

Credits:
School Specialty Children's Publishing Editorial/Art & Design Team
Vincent F. Douglas, *President*
Tracey E. Dils, *Publisher*
Phyllis Sibbing, B.S. Ed., *Project Editor*
Rose Audette, *Art Director*

Also Thanks to:
4ward Communications, Interior Production
Jenny Campbell, Interior Illustration

Send all inquiries to:
School Specialty Children's Publishing
8720 Orion Place
Columbus, OH 43240-2111

ISBN 1-57768-664-0

6 7 8 9 10 11 12 VHG 09 08 07 06 05 04

Table of Contents

Just for Parents

For All Students

Kinds of Questions

Subject Help

Practice Test and Final Test

About the Tests

What Are Standardized Achievement Tests?

Achievement tests measure what children know in particular subject areas such as reading, language arts, and mathematics. They do not measure your child's intelligence or ability to learn.

When tests are standardized, or *normed*, children's test results are compared with those of a specific group who have taken the test, usually at the same age or grade.

Standardized achievement tests measure what children around the country are learning. The test makers survey popular textbook series, as well as state curriculum frameworks and other professional sources, to determine what content is covered widely.

Because of variations in state frameworks and textbook series, as well as grade ranges on some test levels, the tests may cover some material that children have not yet learned. This is especially true if the test is offered early in the school year. However, test scores are compared to those of other children who take the test at the same time of year, so your child will not be at a disadvantage if his or her class has not covered specific material yet.

Different School Districts, Different Tests

There are many flexible options for districts when offering standardized tests. Many school districts choose not to give the full test battery, but select certain content and scoring options. For example, many schools may test only in the areas of reading and mathematics. Similarly, a state or district may use one test for certain grades and another test for other grades. These decisions are often based on the amount of time and money a district wishes to spend on test administration. Some states choose to develop their own statewide assessment tests.

On pages 6 and 7 you will find information about these five widely used standardized achievement tests:

- California Achievement Tests (CAT)
- Terra Nova/CTBS
- Iowa Test of Basic Skills (ITBS)
- Stanford Achievement Test (SAT9)
- Metropolitan Achievement Test (MAT).

However, this book contains strategies and practice questions for use with a variety of tests. Even if your state does not give one of the five tests listed above, your child will benefit from doing the practice questions in this book. If you're unsure about which test your child takes, contact your local school district to find out which tests are given.

Types of Test Questions

Traditionally, standardized achievements tests have used only multiple choice questions. Today, many tests may include constructed response (short answer) and extended response (essay) questions as well.

In addition, many tests include questions that tap students' higher-order thinking skills. Instead of simple recall questions, such as identifying a date in history, questions may require students to make comparisons and contrasts or analyze results among other skills.

What the Tests Measure

These tests do not measure your child's level of intelligence, but they do show how well your child knows material that he or she has learned and that is also covered on the tests. It's important to remember that some tests cover content that is not taught in your child's school or grade. In other instances, depending on when in the year the test is given, your child may not yet have covered the material.

If the test reports you receive show that your child needs improvement in one or more skill areas, you may want to seek help from your child's teacher and find out how you can work with your child to improve his or her skills.

California Achievement Tests (CAT/5)

What Is the California Achievement Test?

The California Achievement Test is a standardized achievement test battery that is widely used with elementary through high school students.

Parts of the Test

The CAT includes tests in the following content areas:

Reading
- Word Analysis
- Vocabulary
- Comprehension

Spelling

Language Arts
- Language Mechanics
- Language Usage

Mathematics

Science

Social Studies

Your child may take some or all of these subtests if your district uses the *California Achievement Test*.

Terra Nova/CTBS (Comprehensive Tests of Basic Skills)

What Is the Terra Nova/CTBS?

The *Terra Nova/Comprehensive Tests of Basic Skills* is a standardized achievement test battery used in elementary through high school grades. While many of the test questions on the *Terra Nova* are in the traditional multiple-choice form, your child may take parts of the *Terra Nova* that include some open-ended questions (constructed-response items).

Parts of the Test

Your child may take some or all of the following subtests if your district uses the *Terra Nova/CTBS*:

Reading/Language Arts
Mathematics
Science
Social Studies

Supplementary tests include:
- Word Analysis
- Vocabulary
- Language Mechanics
- Spelling
- Mathematics Computation

Critical thinking skills may also be tested.

Iowa Tests of Basic Skills (ITBS)

What Is the ITBS?

The *Iowa Test of Basic Skills* is a standardized achievement test battery used in elementary through high school grades.

Parts of the Test

Your child may take some or all of these subtests if your district uses the *ITBS*, also known as the *Iowa*:

Reading
- Vocabulary
- Reading Comprehension

Language Arts
- Spelling
- Capitalization
- Punctuation
- Usage and Expression

Math
- Concepts/Estimate
- Problems/Data Interpretation

Social Studies

Science

Sources of Information

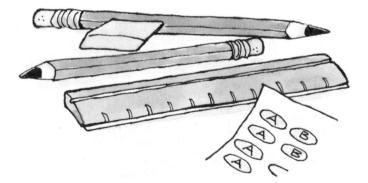

Stanford Achievement Test (SAT9)

What Is the Stanford Achievement Test?

The *Stanford Achievement Test, Ninth Edition (SAT9)* is a standardized achievement test battery used in elementary through high school grades.

Note that the *Stanford Achievement Test (SAT9)* is a different test from the *SAT* used by high school students for college admissions.

While many of the test questions on the *SAT9* are in traditional multiple choice form, your child may take parts of the *SAT9* that include some open-ended questions (constructed-response items).

Parts of the Test

Your child may take some or all of these subtests if your district uses the Stanford Achievement Test.

Reading
- Vocabulary
- Reading Comprehension

Mathematics
- Problem Solving
- Procedures

Language Arts

Spelling

Study Skills

Listening

Critical thinking skills may also be tested.

Metropolitan Achievement Test (MAT7 and MAT8)

What Is the Metropolitan Achievement Test?

The *Metropolitan Achievement Test* is a standardized achievement test battery used in elementary through high school grades.

Parts of the Test

Your child may take some or all of these subtests if your district uses the *Metropolitan Achievement Test.*

Reading
- Vocabulary
- Reading Comprehension

Math
- Concepts and Problem Solving
- Computation

Language Arts
- Pre-writing
- Composing
- Editing

Science

Social Studies

Research Skills

Thinking Skills

Spelling

Statewide Assessments

Today the majority of states give statewide assessments. In some cases these tests are known as *high-stakes assessments.* This means that students must score at a certain level in order to be promoted. Some states use minimum competency or proficiency tests. Often these tests measure more basic skills than other types of statewide assessments.

Statewide assessments are generally linked to state curriculum frameworks. Frameworks provide a blueprint, or outline, to ensure that teachers are covering the same curriculum topics as other teachers in the same grade level in the state. In some states, standardized achievement tests (such as the five described in this book) are used in connection with statewide assessments.

When Statewide Assessments Are Given

Statewide assessments may not be given at every grade level. Generally, they are offered at one or more grades in elementary school, middle school, and high school. Many states test at grades 4, 8, and 10.

State-by-State Information

You can find information about statewide assessments and curriculum frameworks at your state Department of Education Web site. To find the address for your individual state go to www.ed.gov, click on Topics A–Z, and then click on State Departments of Education. You will find a list of all the state departments of education, mailing addresses, and Web sites.

How to Help Your Child Prepare for Standardized Testing

Preparing All Year Round

Perhaps the most valuable way you can help your child prepare for standardized achievement tests is by providing enriching experiences. Keep in mind also, that test results for younger children are not as reliable as for older students. If a child is hungry, tired, or upset, this may result in a poor test score. Here are some tips on how you can help your child do his or her best on standardized tests.

Read aloud with your child. Reading aloud helps develop vocabulary and fosters a positive attitude toward reading. Reading together is one of the most effective ways you can help your child succeed in school.

Share experiences. Baking cookies together, planting a garden, or making a map of your neighborhood are examples of activities that help build skills that are measured on the tests such as sequencing and following directions.

Become informed about your state's testing procedures. Ask about or watch for announcements of meetings that explain about standardized tests and statewide assessments in your school district.

Talk to your child's teacher about your child's individual performance on these state tests during a parent-teacher conference.

Help your child know what to expect. Read and discuss with your child the test-taking tips in this book. Your child can prepare by working through a couple of strategies a day so that no practice session takes too long.

Help your child with his or her regular school assignments. Set up a quiet study area for homework. Supply this area with pencils, paper, markers, a calculator, a ruler, a dictionary, scissors, glue, and so on. Check your child's homework and offer to help if he or she gets stuck. But remember, it's your child's homework, not yours. If you help too much, your child will not benefit from the activity.

Keep in regular contact with your child's teacher. Attend parent-teacher conferences, school functions, PTA or PTO meetings, and school board meetings. This will help you get to know the educators in your district and the families of your child's classmates.

Learn to use computers as an educational resource. If you do not have a computer and Internet access at home, try your local library.

Remember—simply getting your child comfortable with testing procedures and helping him or her know what to expect can improve test scores!

Getting Ready for the Big Day

There are lots of things you can do on or immediately before test day to improve your child's chances of testing success. What's more, these strategies will help your child prepare him or herself for school tests, too, and promote general study skills that can last a lifetime.

Provide a good breakfast on test day.

Instead of sugar cereal, which provides immediate but not long-term energy, have your child eat a breakfast with protein or complex carbohydrates such as an egg, whole grain cereal or toast, or a banana-yogurt shake.

Promote a good night's sleep. A good night's sleep before the test is essential. Try not to overstress the importance of the test. This may cause your child to lose sleep because of anxiety. Doing some exercise after school and having a quiet evening routine will help your child sleep well the night before the test.

Assure your child that he or she is not expected to know all of the answers on the test. Explain that other children in higher grades may take the same test, and that the test may measure things your child has not yet learned in school. Help your child understand that you expect him or her to put forth a good effort—and that this is enough. Your child should not try to cram for these tests. Also avoid threats or bribes; these put undue pressure on children and may interfere with their best performance.

Keep the mood light and offer encouragement. To provide a break on test days, do something fun and special after school— take a walk around the neighborhood, play a game, read a favorite book, or prepare a special snack together. These activities keep your child's mood light—even if the testing sessions have been difficult—and show how much you appreciate your child's effort.

Taking Standardized Tests

No matter what grade you're in, this is information you can use to prepare for standardized tests. Here is what you'll find:

• Test-taking tips and strategies to use on test day and year-round.
• Important terms to know for Language Arts, Reading, Math, Science, and Social Studies.
• A checklist of skills to complete to help you understand what you need to know in Language Arts, Reading Comprehension, Writing, and Math.
• General study/homework tips.

By opening this book, you've already taken your first step towards test success. The rest is easy—all you have to do is get started!

What You Need to Know

There are many things you can do to increase your test success. Here's a list of tips to keep in mind when you take standardized tests—and when you study for them, too.

Keep up with your school work. One way you can succeed in school and on tests is by studying and doing your homework regularly. Studies show that you remember only about one-fifth of what you memorize the night before a test. That's one good reason not to try to learn it all at once! Keeping up with your work throughout the year will help you remember the material better. You also won't be as tired or nervous as if you try to learn everything at once.

Feel your best. One of the ways you can do your best on tests and in school is to make sure your body is ready. To do this, get a good night's sleep each night and eat a healthy breakfast (not sugary cereal that will leave you tired by the middle of the morning). An egg or a milkshake with yogurt and fresh fruit will give you lasting energy. Also, wear comfortable clothes, maybe your lucky shirt or your favorite color on test day. It can't hurt, and it may even keep you relax.

Be prepared. Do practice questions and learn about how standardized tests are organized. Books like this one will help you know what to expect when you take a standardized test.

When you are taking the test, follow the directions. It is important to listen carefully to the directions your teacher gives and to read the written instructions carefully. Words like *not*, *none*, *rarely*, *never*, and *always* are very important in test directions and questions. You may want to circle words like these.

Look at each page carefully before you start answering. In school you usually read a passage and then answer questions about it. But when you take a test, it's helpful to follow a different order.

If you are taking a Reading test, first read the directions. Then read the questions before you read the passage. This way you will know exactly what kind of information to look for as you read. Next, read the passage carefully. Finally, answer the questions.

On math and science tests, look at the labels on graphs and charts. Think about what each graph or chart shows. Questions often will ask you to draw conclusions about the information.

Manage your time. *Time management* means using your time wisely on a test so that you can finish as much of it as possible and do your best. Look over the test or the parts that you are allowed to do at one time. Sometimes you may want to do the easier parts first. This way, if you run out of time before you finish, you will have completed a good chunk of the work.

For tests that have a time limit, notice what time it is when the test begins and figure out when you need to stop. Check a few times as you work through the test to be sure you are making good progress and not spending too much time on any particular section.

You don't have to keep up with everyone else. You may notice other students in the class finishing before you do. Don't worry about this. Everyone works at a different pace. Just keep going, trying not to spend too long on any one question.

Fill in answer sheets properly. Even if you know every answer on a test, you won't do well unless you enter the answers correctly on the answer sheet.

Fill in the entire bubble, but don't spend too much time making it perfect. Make your mark dark, but not so dark that it goes through the paper! And be sure you only choose one answer for each question, even if you are not sure. If you choose two answers, both will be marked as wrong.

It's usually not a good idea to change your answers. Usually your first choice is the right one. Unless you realize that you misread the question, the directions, or some facts in a passage, it's usually safer to stay with your first answer. If you are pretty sure it's wrong, of course, go ahead and change it. Make sure you completely erase the first choice and neatly fill in your new choice.

Use context clues to figure out tough questions. If you come across a word or idea you don't understand, use context clues—the words in the sentences nearby— to help you figure out its meaning.

Sometimes it's good to guess. Should you guess when you don't know an answer on a test? That depends. If your teacher has made the test, usually you will score better if you answer as many questions as possible, even if you don't really know the answers.

On standardized tests, here's what to do to score your best. For each question, most of these tests let you choose from four or five answer choices. If you decide that a couple of answers are clearly wrong but you're still not sure about the answer, go ahead and make your best guess. If you can't narrow down the choices at all, then you may be better off skipping the question. Tests like these take away extra points for wrong answers, so it's better to leave them blank. Be sure you skip over the answer space for these questions on the answer sheet, though, so you don't fill in the wrong spaces.

Sometimes you should skip a question and come back to it later.

On many tests, you will score better if you answer more questions. This means that you should not spend too much time on any single question. Sometimes it gets tricky, though, keeping track of questions you skipped on your answer sheet.

If you want to skip a question because you don't know the answer, put a very light pencil mark next to the question in the test booklet. Try to choose an answer, even if you're not sure of it. Fill in the answer lightly on the answer sheet.

Check your work. On a standardized test, you can't go ahead or skip back to another section of the test. But you may go back and review your answers on the section you just worked on if you have extra time.

First, scan your answer sheet. Make sure that you answered every question you could. Also, if you are using a bubble-type answer sheet, make sure that you filled in only one bubble for each question. Erase any extra marks on the page.

Finally—avoid test anxiety! If you get nervous about tests, don't worry. *Test anxiety* happens to lots of good students. Being a little nervous actually sharpens your mind. But if you get very nervous about tests, take a few minutes to relax the night before or the day of the test. One good way to relax is to get some exercise, even if you just have time to stretch, shake out your fingers, and wiggle your toes. If you can't move around, it helps just to take a few slow, deep breaths and picture yourself doing a great job!

Terms to Know

Here's a list of terms that are good to know when taking standardized tests. Don't be worried if you see something new. You may not have learned it in school yet.

acute angle: an angle of less than 90°

adjective: a word that describes a noun (*yellow duckling, new bicycle*)

adverb: a word that describes a verb (*ran fast, laughing heartily*)

analogy: a comparison of the relationship between two or more otherwise unrelated things (*Carrot is to vegetable as banana is to fruit.*)

angle: the figure formed by two lines that start at the same point, usually shown in degrees

antonyms: words with opposite meanings (*big* and *small, young* and *old*)

area: the amount of space inside a flat shape, expressed in square units

article: a word such as *a*, *an*, or *the* that goes in front of a noun (*the chicken, an apple*)

cause/effect: the reason that something happens

character: a person in a story, book, movie, play, or TV show

compare/contrast: to tell what is alike and different about two or more things

compass rose: the symbol on a map that shows where North, South, East, and West are

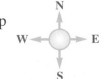

conclusion: a logical decision you can make based on information from a reading selection or science experiment

congruent: equal in size or shape

context clues: language and details in a piece of writing that can help you figure out difficult words and ideas

denominator: in a fraction, the number under the line; shows how many equal parts a whole has been divided into ($\frac{1}{2}$, $\frac{6}{7}$)

direct object: in a sentence, the person or thing that receives the action of a verb (*Jane hit the ball hard.*)

equation: in math, a statement where one set of numbers or values is equal to another set (*6 + 6 = 12, 4 x 5 = 20*)

factor: a whole number that can be divided exactly into another whole number (*1, 2, 3, 4, and 6 are all factors of 12.*)

genre: a category of literature that contains writing with common features (*drama, fiction, nonfiction, poetry*)

hypothesis: in science, the possible answer to a question, most science experiments begin with a hypothesis

indirect object: in a sentence, the noun or pronoun that tells to or for whom the action of the verb is done (*Louise gave a flower to her sister.*)

infer: to make an educated guess about a piece of writing, based on information contained in the selection and what you already know

main idea: the most important idea or message in a writing selection

map legend: the part of a map showing symbols that represent natural or human-made objects

noun: a person, place, or thing (*president, underground, train*)

numerator: in a fraction, the number above the line; shows how many equal parts are to be taken from the denominator ($\frac{3}{4}$, $\frac{1}{5}$)

operation: in math, tells what must be done to numbers in an equation (such as add, subtract, multiply, or divide)

parallel: lines or rays that, if extended, could never intersect

percent: fraction of a whole that has been divided into 100 parts, usually expressed with % sign ($\frac{5}{100} = 5\%$)

perimeter: distance around an object or shape

Perimeter =
3 + 3 + 3 + 3 = 12 ft.

3 ft.
3 ft.   3 ft.
3 ft.

perpendicular: lines or rays that intersect to form a 90° (right) angle

90°

predicate: in a sentence, the word or words that tell what the subject does, did, or has (*The fuzzy kitten had black spots on its belly.*)

predict: in science or reading, to use given information to decide what will happen

prefixes/suffixes: letters added to the beginning or end of a word to change its meaning (*reorganize, hopeless*)

preposition: a word that shows the relationship between a noun or pronoun and other words in a phrase or sentence (*We sat by the fire. She walked through the door.*)

probability: the likelihood that something will happen, often shown with numbers

pronoun: a word that is used in place of a noun (*She gave the present to them.*)

ratio: a comparison of two quantities, often shown as a fraction (*The ratio of boys to girls in the class is 2 to 1, or 2/1.*)

sequence: the order in which events happen or in which items can be placed in a pattern

subject: in a sentence, the word or words that tell who or what the sentence is about (*Uncle Robert baked the cake. Everyone at the party ate it.*)

summary: a restatement of important ideas from a selection in the writer's own words

symmetry: in math and science, two or more sides or faces of an object that are mirror images of one another

line of symmetry

synonyms: words with the same, or almost the same, meaning (*delicious* and *tasty*, *funny* and *comical*)

Venn diagram: two or more overlapping circles used to compare and contrast two or more things

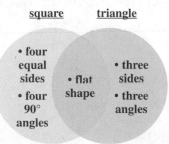

square   triangle

• four equal sides
• four 90° angles

• flat shape

• three sides
• three angles

verb: a word that describes an action or state of being (*He watched the fireworks.*)

writing prompt: on a test, a question or statement that you must respond to in writing

Skills Checklist

Which subjects do you need more practice in? Use the following checklist to find out. Put a check mark next to each statement that is true for you. Then use the unchecked statements to figure out which skills you need to review.

Keep in mind that if you are using these checklists in the middle of the school year, you may not have learned some skills yet. Talk to your teacher or a parent if you need help with a new skill.

Reading

❑ I can use context clues to figure out tough words.

❑ I know what synonyms are and how to use them.

❑ I can find words with opposite meanings.

❑ I can find the main idea or theme of a passage.

❑ I can figure out the author's purpose for writing a passage.

❑ I can predict what will happen next in a story.

❑ I can identify the setting of a story.

Language Arts

I can identify the different parts of speech.

❑ possessive nouns

❑ subject and object pronouns

❑ prepositions

❑ verbs

❑ verb tenses (past, present, and future)

❑ adjectives

❑ adverbs

- ☐ articles

- ☐ contractions

- ☐ prefixes and suffixes

- ☐ I can tell the difference between a complete and an incomplete sentence.

Writing

<u>Before I write</u>

- ☐ I think about who my audience is.

- ☐ I think about my purpose for writing
  (to persuade, inform, entertain, or describe).

<u>When I write a draft</u>

- ☐ I use paragraphs that have a main idea and supporting details.

- ☐ I use words and actions that tell about my characters.

- ☐ I include details that tell about the setting.

- ☐ I use reference materials (encyclopedias, dictionaries, the Internet)
  to find information.

<u>As I revise my work</u>

- ☐ I check for spelling, capitalization, punctuation, and grammar mistakes.

- ☐ I take out parts that aren't necessary.

- ☐ I add words and sentences to make my work more interesting.

- ☐ I neatly write or type my final copy.

- ☐ I include my name and a title on the finished work.

Mathematics

Number Sense

❑ I can recognize and use place value to the millions place.

❑ I can round numbers to the nearest ten, hundred, and thousand.

Addition and Subtraction

❑ I can add and subtract two- and three-digit numbers and greater.

❑ I can add and subtract decimals to the tenths and hundredths places.

Multiplication and Division

❑ I can multiply by one- and two-digit numbers.

❑ I can divide two- and three-digit numbers.

❑ I can regroup when multiplying with one-, two-, and three-digit numbers.

Measurement

I can estimate and measure using the standard units for

❑ length (inch, foot, yard, mile).

❑ weight (ounce, pound, ton).

❑ capacity (cup, pint, quart, gallon).

❑ time (seconds, minutes, hours).

I can estimate and measure using the metric units for

❑ length (centimeter, decimeter, meter, kilometer).

❑ mass (gram, kilogram).

❑ capacity (milliliter, liter).

❑ I can solve simple problems with units of time, length, weight/mass, and capacity.

Fractions

- ❑ I can compare equivalent fractions.
- ❑ I can add and subtract fractions.
- ❑ I can solve problems with mixed numbers.

Geometry

I can identify

- ❑ polygons.
- ❑ lines, line segments, and rays.
- ❑ angles.

Problem Solving

- ❑ When I do number problems, I read the directions carefully.
- ❑ When I do word problems, I read the problems carefully.
- ❑ I look for words that tell the operation I must use to solve the problem.
- ❑ I label my answer with units when necessary.

I use different strategies to solve different kinds of problems:

- ❑ I estimate and use mental math.
- ❑ I make pictures, diagrams, and charts.
- ❑ I look for patterns.
- ❑ I can read and construct pictographs, line graphs, and bar graphs.

Preparing All Year Round

Believe it or not, knowing how to study and manage your time is a skill you will use for the rest of your life. There are helpful strategies that you can use to be more successful in school. The following is a list of tips to keep in mind as you study for tests and school assignments.

Get organized. To make it easy to get your homework done, set up a place in which to do it each day. Choose a location where you can give the work your full attention. Find a corner of your room, the kitchen, or another quiet place where you won't be interrupted. Put all the tools you'll need in that area. Set aside a drawer or basket for school supplies. That way you won't have to go hunting each time you need a sharp pencil! Here are some things you may want to keep in your study corner for homework and school projects:

- pencils and pens
- pencil sharpener
- notebook paper
- tape
- glue
- scissors
- crayons, markers, colored pencils
- stapler
- construction paper, printer paper
- dictionary

Schedule your assignments. The best way to keep track of homework and special projects is by planning and managing your time. Keep a schedule of homework assignments and other events to help you get organized. Make your own or make a copy of the **Homework Log and Weekly Schedule** provided on pages 22–23 of this book for each week you're in school.

Record your homework assignments on the log as completely as you can. Enter the book, page number, and exercise number of each assignment. Enter dates of tests as soon as you know them so that you can begin to study ahead of time. Study a section of the material each day. Then review all of it the day before the test.

Also make notes to help you remember special events and materials such as permission slips you need to return. List after-school activities so you can plan your homework and study time around them. Remember to record fun activities on your log, too. You don't want to forget that party you've been invited to or even just time you'd like to spend hanging out or studying with friends.

Do your homework right away. Set aside a special time every day after school to do your homework. You may want to take a break when you first get home, but give yourself plenty of time to do your homework, too. That way you won't get interrupted by dinner or get too tired to finish.

If you are bored or confused by an assignment and you really don't want to do it, promise yourself a little reward, perhaps a snack or 15 minutes of playing ball after you've really worked hard for 45 minutes or so. Then go back to work for a while if you need to, and take another break later.

Get help if you need it. If you need help, just ask. Call a friend or ask a family member for help. If these people can't help you, be sure to ask your teacher the next day about any work you didn't understand.

Use a computer. If you have one available, a computer can be a great tool for doing homework. Typing your homework on the computer lets you hand in neat papers, check your spelling easily, and look up the definitions of words you aren't sure about. If you have an Internet connection, you can also do research without leaving home.

Before you go online, talk with your family about ways to stay safe. Be sure never to give out personal information (your name, age, address, or phone number) without permission.

Practice, practice, practice! The best way to improve your skills in specific subject areas is through lots of practice. If you have trouble in a school subject such as math, science, social studies, language arts, or reading, doing some extra activities or projects can give you just the boost you need.

Homework Log
and Weekly Schedule

	Monday	Tuesday	Wednesday
MATH			
SOCIAL STUDIES			
SCIENCE			
READING			
LANGUAGE ARTS			
OTHER			

for the week of _____

Thursday	Friday	Saturday/Sunday	
			MATH
			SOCIAL STUDIES
			SCIENCE
			READING
			LANGUAGE ARTS
			OTHER

What's Ahead in This Book?

As you know, you will have to take many tests while in school. But there is no reason to be nervous about taking standardized tests. You can prepare for them by doing your best in school all year. You can also learn about the types of questions you'll see on standardized tests and helpful strategies for answering the questions. That's what this book is all about. It has been developed especially to help you and other fourth graders know what to expect—and what to do—on test day.

The first section will introduce you to the different kinds of questions found on most standardized tests. Multiple choice, short answer, matching, and other types of questions will be explained in detail. You'll get tips for answering each type. Then you'll be given sample questions to work through so you can practice your skills.

Next, you'll find sections on these major school subjects: reading, language arts, math, social studies (sometimes called citizenship), and science. You'll discover traps to watch for in each subject area and tricks you can use to make answering the questions easier. And there are plenty of practice questions provided to sharpen your skills even more.

Finally, you'll find two sections of questions. One is called Short Practice and the other is called Full Practice. The questions are designed to look just like the ones you'll be given in school on a real standardized test. An answer key is at the back of the book so you can check your own answers. Once you check your answers, you can see in which subject areas you need more practice.

So good luck—test success is just around the corner!

Multiple Choice Questions

You have probably seen multiple choice questions before. They are the most common type of question used on standardized tests. To answer a multiple choice question, you must choose one answer from a number of choices.

EXAMPLE   **The word that means the opposite of <u>rapid</u> is _____ .**

Ⓐ shallow   Ⓒ speedy

Ⓑ sluggish   Ⓓ rabbit

Sometimes you will know the answer right away. Other times you won't. To answer multiple choice questions on a test, do the following:

• Read the directions carefully. If you're not sure what you're supposed to do, you might make a lot of mistakes.

• First answer any easy questions whose answers you are *sure* you know.

• When you come to a harder question, circle the question number. You can come back to this question after you have finished all the easier ones.

• When you're ready to answer a hard question, throw out answers that you know are wrong. You can do this by making an **X** after each choice you know is not correct. The last choice left is probably the correct one.

Testing It Out

Now look at the sample question more closely.

Think: I know that rapid means "fast." So I must be looking for a word that means "slow." I have already eliminated *speedy* and *rabbit*. *Speedy* has the same meaning as *rapid*. *Rabbit* doesn't really have anything to do with *rapid*.

Now I have to choose between *shallow* and *sluggish*. *Shallow* means the opposite of *deep*, not the opposite of *fast*. I do not know the word *sluggish*, but I do know that slugs are slow-moving creatures. So I will choose **B**.

Multiple Choice Practice

Directions: For questions 1–3, find the word that means the *opposite* of the underlined word.

1 The tortoise took a <u>leisurely</u> walk.

  Ⓐ lovely

  Ⓑ swift

  Ⓒ leathery

  Ⓓ delicious

2 Gazelles and impalas are <u>prey</u> to the cheetah.

  Ⓕ food

  Ⓖ friends

  Ⓗ similar

  Ⓙ predators

3 Banana slugs are <u>moist</u> to the touch.

  Ⓐ dry

  Ⓑ slimy

  Ⓒ rough

  Ⓓ rubbery

Directions: For questions 4-6, find the word that rhymes or almost rhymes with the underlined syllable.

4 animals repro<u>duce</u>

  Ⓕ stuck

  Ⓖ choose

  Ⓗ moose

  Ⓙ much

5 swift carni<u>vore</u>

  Ⓐ oar

  Ⓑ hour

  Ⓒ scar

  Ⓓ warn

6 <u>ar</u>id desert

  Ⓕ here

  Ⓖ fair

  Ⓗ here?

  Ⓙ far

Fill-in-the-Blank Questions

On some tests, you will be given multiple choice questions where you must fill in something that's missing from a phrase, sentence, equation, or passage. These are called "fill-in-the-blank" questions.

EXAMPLE   **Pablo was looking _____ to his family's camping trip.**

   Ⓐ foremost   Ⓒ former

   Ⓑ forehead   Ⓓ forward

To answer fill-in-the-blank questions, do the following:

- First read the item with a blank that needs to be filled.
- See if you can think of the answer even before you look at your choices.
- Even if the answer you first thought of is one of the choices, be sure to check the other choices. There may be an even better answer.
- For harder questions, try to fit every answer choice into the blank. Underline clue words that may help you find the correct answer. Write an **X** after answers that do not fit. Choose the answer that does fit. You can also use this strategy to double-check your answers.

Testing It Out

Now look at the sample question more closely.

 **Think:** "Pablo was looking _____ to his family's camping trip." If I were going on a camping trip, I would probably be excited about it—looking forward to it. Maybe one of the choices is *forward*. Yes, it is—the answer must be **D**.

To double-check, I'll try the other answer choices in the sentence. None of them makes sense: "looking foremost," "looking forehead," and "looking former" all sound wrong. Answer **D** still seems correct to me.

Fill-in-the-Blank Practice

Directions: Find the word that best completes each sentence.

1 Pablo's family drove up the mountain on a long, _____ road.

Ⓐ wind

Ⓑ windshield

Ⓒ winding

Ⓓ whiny

2 Finally they _____ at the campground.

Ⓕ landed

Ⓖ embarked

Ⓗ left

Ⓙ arrived

3 Each campsite had a food locker to _____ visits from hungry bears.

Ⓐ encourage

Ⓑ arrange

Ⓒ discourage

Ⓓ promote

4 _____ , Mom had forgotten the can opener.

Ⓕ Fortunately

Ⓖ Mournfully

Ⓗ Excitedly

Ⓙ Unfortunately

5 They were _____ to eat marshmallows and chocolate bars for dinner!

Ⓐ forced

Ⓑ intrigued

Ⓒ chosen

Ⓓ ordered

6 Carmina _____ left a chocolate bar on the camp table.

Ⓕ carefully

Ⓖ carelessly

Ⓗ calmly

Ⓙ merrily

True/False Questions

A true/false question asks you to read a statement and decide if it is right (true) or wrong (false). Sometimes you will be asked to write **T** for true or **F** for false. Most of the time you must fill in a bubble next to the correct answer.

EXAMPLE | **It is important to eat a good breakfast.**

     Ⓐ   true

     Ⓑ   false

To answer true/false questions on a test, think about the following:

- True/false sections contain more questions than other sections of a test. If there is a time limit on the test, you may need to go a little more quickly than usual. Do not spend too much time on any one question.
- First answer all of the easy questions. Circle the numbers next to harder ones and come back to them later.
- If you have time left after completing all the questions, quickly double-check your answers.
- True/false questions with words like *always*, *never*, *none*, *only*, and *every* are usually false. This is because they limit a statement so much.
- True-false questions with words like *most*, *many*, and *generally* are often true. This is because they make statements more believable.

Testing It Out

Now look at the sample question more closely.

 Think: Is it important to eat a good breakfast? Yes, I've heard that before. I don't see any words like *always*, *never*, or *every* to limit the statement. My first instinct must be right. I'll choose **T** for true.

True/False Practice

Directions: Decide if each statement is true or false.

1 Oranges, lemons, and grapefruits are citrus fruits.

Ⓐ true Ⓑ false

2 Everyone drinks orange juice for breakfast.

Ⓐ true Ⓑ false

3 No one drinks lemonade for breakfast.

Ⓐ true Ⓑ false

4 Many people drink citrus juices for breakfast.

Ⓐ true Ⓑ false

5 Pineapples are grown in Hawaii.

Ⓐ true Ⓑ false

6 Hawaii is the only place where pineapples grow.

Ⓐ true Ⓑ false

7 Fresh strawberries are always available at the supermarket.

Ⓐ true Ⓑ false

8 You can usually buy strawberries at the supermarket.

Ⓐ true Ⓑ false

9 All children like fruits better than vegetables.

Ⓐ true Ⓑ false

10 Everyone dislikes vegetables.

Ⓐ true Ⓑ false

11 Some vegetables are used to make desserts.

Ⓐ true Ⓑ false

12 Everyone eats pumpkin pie on Thanksgiving.

Ⓐ true Ⓑ false

Matching Questions

Matching questions ask you to find pairs of words or phrases that go together. The choices are often shown in columns.

Match items that mean the same, or almost the same, thing.

1 interest	A distress	1	Ⓐ Ⓑ Ⓒ Ⓓ
2 discourage	B cheer up	2	Ⓐ Ⓑ Ⓒ Ⓓ
3 encourage	C fascinate	3	Ⓐ Ⓑ Ⓒ Ⓓ
4 worry	D disappoint	4	Ⓐ Ⓑ Ⓒ Ⓓ

When answering matching questions on tests, follow these guidelines:

• Match the easiest choices first.
• If you come to a word you don't know, look for prefixes, suffixes, or root words to help figure out its meaning. Also, try using it in a sentence.
• Work down one column at a time. It is confusing to switch back and forth.

Testing It Out

Now look at the sample question more closely.

Think: I'll start with the first column. *Interest* is a word I've seen before. I think that *fascinate* means the same thing as, so I'll choose **C** to go with number 1.

I know that *disappointed* is the way people feel when they don't get something they want. *Let down* means the same thing. So I'll choose **D**.

I think that *support* might mean something similar to *help*. Let's see— "My mom gave me all the help she could." "My mom gave me all the support she could." Yes, both sentences make sense. I'll choose **B**.

The fourth word is *worry*. The only remaining choice is *distress*, but I don't know what it means. It might have something to do with being upset, but the only other possible word is *disappoint*, and I'm sure of my choice for that word. So I'll choose **A**.

Matching Practice

Directions: For numbers 1–16, match words or phrases with opposite meanings.

1	dark	A	petite	1	Ⓐ Ⓑ Ⓒ Ⓓ
2	large	B	silky	2	Ⓐ Ⓑ Ⓒ Ⓓ
3	rough	C	immobile	3	Ⓐ Ⓑ Ⓒ Ⓓ
4	active	D	pale	4	Ⓐ Ⓑ Ⓒ Ⓓ

5	fall asleep	F	cease	5	Ⓕ Ⓖ Ⓗ Ⓙ
6	proceed	G	awaken	6	Ⓕ Ⓖ Ⓗ Ⓙ
7	grin	H	weep	7	Ⓕ Ⓖ Ⓗ Ⓙ
8	giggle	J	scowl	8	Ⓕ Ⓖ Ⓗ Ⓙ

9	starving	A	exhausted	9	Ⓐ Ⓑ Ⓒ Ⓓ
10	wide awake	B	thrilled	10	Ⓐ Ⓑ Ⓒ Ⓓ
11	discouraged	C	full	11	Ⓐ Ⓑ Ⓒ Ⓓ
12	intrigued	D	bored	12	Ⓐ Ⓑ Ⓒ Ⓓ

13	clear up	F	sprint	13	Ⓕ Ⓖ Ⓗ Ⓙ
14	take	G	succeed	14	Ⓕ Ⓖ Ⓗ Ⓙ
15	fail	H	confuse	15	Ⓕ Ⓖ Ⓗ Ⓙ
16	crawl	J	give	16	Ⓕ Ⓖ Ⓗ Ⓙ

Analogy Questions

Analogies are a special kind of question. In an analogy question, you are asked to figure out the relationship between two things. Then you must complete another pair with the same relationship.

EXAMPLE   **Porcupine is to quills as bee is to _____ .**

    Ⓐ sharp   Ⓒ buzzing

    Ⓑ insect   Ⓓ stinger

Analogies usually have two pairs of items. In the question above, the two pairs are *porcupine/quills* and *bee/ _____* . To answer analogy questions on standardized tests, do the following:

• Try to form a sentence that explains how they are related.
• Next, use your sentence to figure out the missing word in the second pair of items.
• For more difficult analogies, try each answer choice in the sentence you formed. Choose the answer that fits best.

Testing It Out
Now look at the sample question more closely.

Think: How are *porcupine* and *quills* related? A porcupine has quills on its body; it uses its quills to protect itself. So if I use the word *bee* in this sentence, I'd say, "A bee has a _____ on its body; it uses its _____ to protect itself."

Choice **A** is *sharp*. If I use *sharp* to complete the sentence, I end up with, *A bee has sharp on its body; it uses its sharp to protect itself.* That makes no sense.

Choice **B** is *insect*. If I use *insect* to complete the sentence, I end up with *A bee has an insect on its body; it uses its insect to protect itself.* That makes no sense, either.

Choice **C** is *buzzing*. *A bee has a buzzing on its body; it uses its buzzing to protect itself.* Bees do buzz, but they don't have *buzzing* on their body.

Choice **D** is *stinger*. *A bee has a stinger on its body; it uses its stinger to protect itself.* Yes, both parts of that sentence are true. **D** is the correct choice.

Analogy Practice

Directions: Find the word that best completes each analogy.

1 <u>Artist</u> is to <u>paintbrush</u> as <u>carpenter</u> is to _____ .

Ⓐ hammer

Ⓑ worker

Ⓒ computer

Ⓓ building

2 <u>Gigantic</u> is to <u>big</u> as <u>miniscule</u> is to _____ .

Ⓕ gargantuan

Ⓖ little

Ⓗ infinite

Ⓙ mouse

3 <u>January</u> is to <u>February</u> as <u>Monday</u> is to _____ .

Ⓐ Thursday

Ⓑ Sunday

Ⓒ March

Ⓓ Tuesday

4 <u>Sweltering</u> is to <u>freezing</u> as <u>hot</u> is to _____ .

Ⓕ weather

Ⓖ ice

Ⓗ cold

Ⓙ boiling

5 <u>Syrup</u> is to <u>pancakes</u> as <u>butter</u> is to _____ .

Ⓐ peanut butter

Ⓑ bread

Ⓒ baking

Ⓓ milk

6 <u>People</u> is to <u>person</u> as <u>children</u> is to _____ .

Ⓕ smaller

Ⓖ baby

Ⓗ adults

Ⓙ child

Short Answer Questions

Some test questions don't give you answers to choose from; instead, you must write short answers in your own words. These are called "short answer" or "open response" questions.

EXAMPLE   Ted saw that a rowboat had tipped over and two people were struggling in the water. He swam out to the boat. He calmed the two swimmers and showed them how to hold on to the overturned boat. Then he stayed with them until a rescue boat could get there.

1. What word or words would you use to describe Ted? _____

2. How do you think the people in the water felt about Ted? _____

When you must write short answers to questions on a standardized test, do the following:

• Read each question carefully. Make sure to respond directly to the question that is being asked.

• Your response should be short but complete.

• Write in complete sentences unless the directions say you don't have to.

• Make sure to double-check your answers for spelling, punctuation, and grammar when you are done.

Testing It Out

Now reread the paragraph about Ted and the questions.

Think: From the story, I can tell that Ted is brave. He tried to save the swimmers even though it might have been dangerous. I know he is a good swimmer because he stayed in the water for a long time and showed the swimmers how to hold on to the boat. Even though the directions don't say, I know I should write in complete sentences. So I'll write:

1. *Ted is brave. He is also a good swimmer.*

The swimmers must have appreciated Ted's help. So I'll write:

2. *The swimmers were glad that Ted was there to help them.*

Short Answer Practice

Directions: For questions 1 and 2, look at the diagrams and answer the questions.

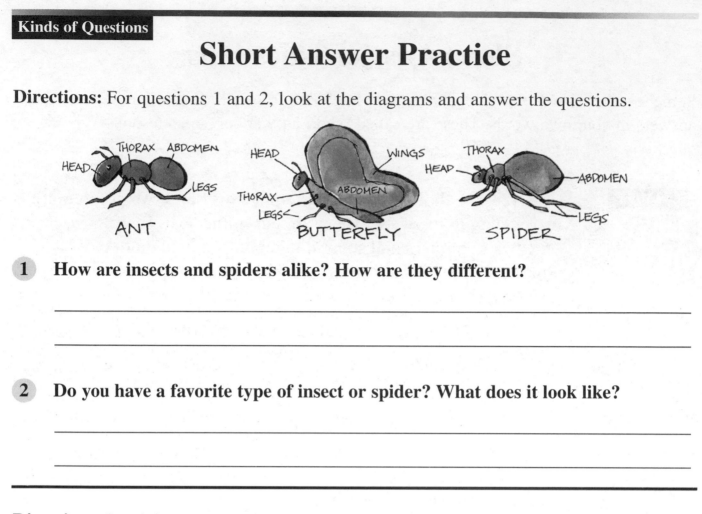

1 How are insects and spiders alike? How are they different?

_____

_____

2 Do you have a favorite type of insect or spider? What does it look like?

_____

_____

Directions: Read the passage below. Then answer questions 3 and 4.

Jack woke up suddenly. He heard someone digging around the edge of his tent. He lay quietly, thinking about the bears and mountain lions that lived in the forest. What should he do? Suddenly, a hand reached into the tent and grabbed his backpack. "Hi, Jack," said his brother Matt. "I was hoping you still had some of that trail mix. We're all hungry in my tent." Jack groaned and turned over to go back to sleep.

3 What do you think Jack feels when he first wakes up? How were his feelings different at the end of the passage?

_____

_____

4 Do you agree with Matt's behavior? Why or why not?

_____

_____

Reading

Many standardized tests have sections called "Reading" or "Reading Comprehension." Reading Comprehension questions test your ability to read for detail, find meaning in a sentence or passage, and use context clues to figure out words or ideas you don't understand. The following is a list of topics covered on Reading Comprehension tests.

Word Meaning

Word meaning questions test your vocabulary and your ability to figure out unfamiliar words. When answering questions about word meaning:

- See if you can find prefixes, suffixes, or root words for clues to their meaning.
- Look at the other words in the sentence or passage to help tell what the underlined word means.

When the climbers reached the summit, they could see for miles.

The underlined word must mean "top" or "peak."

Characterization

What characters say, do, and feel is an important part of many reading passages.

When Jennie heard the news, she made a face and groaned.

Is Jennie happy about the news? No, her actions tell you she is unhappy.

Cause and Effect

Look for **cause and effect** when you read. A **cause** is an event that makes another one happen. The **effect** is the event that is caused.

- Words like *before*, *after*, and *because* can provide clues to cause and effect.
- Sometimes you must use context clues and what you already know to figure out the cause or effect of something.

Louis's grandmother was furious. "I told you not to swim in the pool without and adult nearby! I'm afraid you can't go to the movies tonight."

We can assume that Louis's grandmother is furious because he went in the pool without an adult nearby. We can also assume that she won't let him go to the movies for the same reason.

Sequence

The **sequence of events** is the order in which events take place.

- Look for clue words such as first, next, last, finally, before, and after to help you tell the sequence of events in a story.
- Sometimes the events in a story won't be listed in sequence. Then you have to read carefully for other clues to the sequence.

First, you mix the ingredients. Then, you roll the cookies into little balls. Next, you place the cookie sheet into the oven. Finally, they are done and ready to eat!

Reading Practice

Directions: Read the passage and then answer the questions.

Mario walked back and forth at the end of the pool. This was his chance. He had been practicing his dives for months now and today he would have a chance to show what he had learned.

Suddenly Dave walked into the pool enclosure. He strutted over to Mario and said, "Well, my friend, do you think you can win today? I doubt it, because I've won all the diving contests in the last three years. But you can go ahead and try, if you want to."

Mario felt a lump in his throat. Dave was the one person he would have a hard time beating. Mario had always respected Dave's ability to dive, but hated his attitude. Mario had talent, too, and he didn't walk around as if he were the king of the pool!

"Take your places," said the announcer over the loudspeaker. Mario moved to the edge of the pool and knelt in position. He moved back from the edge of the pool and knelt in place. The first dive would be the racing dive. He could see Dave out of the corner of his eye. Dave had an annoying smirk on his face as he took his position. Mario took a deep breath and waited for the starting pistol.

1 **Which word best describes Dave?**

(A) puzzled

(B) conceited

(C) unsure

(D) friendly

2 **Which word from the passage means about the same thing as talent?**

(F) position

(G) attitude

(H) ability

(J) enclosure

3 **What does smirk mean?**

(A) friendly smile

(B) scar

(C) smug expression

(D) face mask

4 **What does strutted mean?**

(F) walked in a bragging manner

(G) walked on tiptoe

(H) walked in circles

(J) walked without confidence

Language Arts

Language Mechanics and Expression

Standardized tests usually include questions about spelling, grammar, punctuation, and capitalization. These questions are often grouped together in sections called "Language Mechanics and Expression" or "Language Arts."

The following is a list of different topics included under Language Mechanics and Expression. Look at the tips and examples that go with each topic. If you have trouble with one of the topics listed, talk to a teacher or parent about getting extra help.

Grammar

Grammar is the set of rules that helps you write good, clear sentences. Whether you are answering a multiple choice question, writing a short answer, or responding to a writing prompt, you should:

- Be sure the subject and verb of each sentence agree with one another.

Daryl | usually | wins | the class
singular subject   *singular verb*

spelling bee.

Daryl and Linda | usually | win | the class
plural subject   *plural verb*

spelling bee.

- Remember how to use different parts of speech such as nouns, verbs, adjectives, adverbs, pronouns, and conjunctions.

Sam | studies | constantly. | He | is | an |
noun   *verb*   *adverb*   *pronoun* *verb* *article*

amazing | student | and | always | gets | A's.
adjective   *noun* *conjunction* *adverb*   *verb*   *noun*

Capitalization

You may be asked to identify words that should be capitalized and words that shouldn't. Remember:

- Always capitalize the first word in a sentence.
- Always capitalize the names of people, places, and other proper nouns.

My friend Chow celebrates Chinese New Year.

On the other hand, Alana and Lakeisha celebrate Kwanzaa.

- Capitalize proper adjectives.

We went out for Vietnamese food on my mother's birthday.

Punctuation

You will probably be given multiple choice questions about punctuation, but you will also be required to use punctuation marks when you write answers in your own words.

- Make sure to check punctuation at the end of sentences and within them.

> The wind just blew the maple tree down!
>
> Did it hit the house?
>
> No, we were lucky.
>
> It's blocking the street; we should call city services.

Spelling

You may be asked to pick out misspelled words or choose the correct spelling of a word that is already misspelled. You should also check your own spelling when you write.

> The ship saled across the see.
>
> The ship sailed across the sea.

- If you're taking a test and you're not sure which answer choice is correct, try spelling out the word on scrap paper. If your spelling matches one of the answer choices, it is probably correct.

Sentence Structure

Remember to use complete sentences whenever you write a short answer or paragraph. To tell if a sentence is complete:

- Make sure the sentence has a subject and a verb.
- Make sure the sentence starts with a capital letter and ends with the correct punctuation mark.

> Blew in from the west.
> (verb only: incorrect)
>
> A fierce storm blew in from the west.
> (subject and verb: correct)

Also keep in mind:
- Avoid beginning sentences with *And*.
- You can often make two sentences more interesting by combining them. To do this, you can use conjunctions such as *and*, *but*, *so*, or *however*. You can also combine sentences with punctuation marks such as commas and semicolons. However, you must be careful not to change the meaning of the sentences you are combining.

> The Majors have a dog. The Wyatts have a dog. My family has always liked cats. [short uncombined sentences]
>
> The Majors and the Wyatts have dogs, but my family has always liked cats. [short sentences combined into one]

Language Arts

Directions: Choose the punctuation that is missing from numbers 1–3.

1 **Do you think the film is scary__**

.   ,   ?   !
Ⓐ   Ⓑ   Ⓒ   Ⓓ

2 **It__s more funny than scary.**

?   ,   .   ,
Ⓕ   Ⓖ   Ⓗ   Ⓙ

3 **Lookout, here comes an avalanche__**

!   .   ?   ,
Ⓐ   Ⓑ   Ⓒ   Ⓓ

Directions: For question 4, choose the correct capitalized sentence.

4 **i took jake's dog ben for a walk.**

Ⓕ I took Jake's dog ben for a walk.

Ⓖ I took jake's dog Ben for a walk.

Ⓗ I took Jake's Dog ben for a walk.

Ⓙ I took Jake's dog Ben for a walk.

Directions: For questions 5–7, choose the verb that best completes each sentence.

5 **Mr. Jacobs _____ the school band.**

Ⓐ leading

Ⓑ lead

Ⓒ leads

Ⓓ are leading

6 **The horn players _____ in the city finals.**

Ⓕ competes

Ⓖ is competing

Ⓗ compete

Ⓙ competing

7 **My mother _____ for three hours.**

Ⓐ drive

Ⓑ driven

Ⓒ has drove

Ⓓ drove

Directions: For questions 8-11, choose the correctly spelled word.

8 **We need a new _____ _____.**

 Ⓕ vidio recorder

 Ⓖ video recordor

 Ⓗ video recorder

 Ⓙ vidio ricorder

9 **"That closet needs a _____ cleaning!" my Mom said.**

 Ⓐ thorogh

 Ⓑ thurough

 Ⓒ thurogh

 Ⓓ thorough

10 **My teacher _____ that I practice my violin for one hour each day.**

 Ⓕ recommended

 Ⓖ reccommended

 Ⓗ reccomended

 Ⓙ recomended

11 **Alexa sure was _____ about visiting her Grandma!**

 Ⓐ exited

 Ⓑ excited

 Ⓒ exsited

 Ⓓ ecsited

Directions: Answer question 12.

12 **Which of the following is not a complete sentence?**

 Ⓕ Simon pitched for the Eagles on Sunday.

 Ⓖ Simon the Eagles on Sunday.

 Ⓗ On Sunday, Simon pitched for the Eagles.

 Ⓙ Simon pitched.

Directions: For question 13, choose the best combined sentence.

13 **The traffic was loud. The neighbors were loud. I couldn't sleep.**

 Ⓐ The traffic was loud and the neighbors were loud. I couldn't sleep.

 Ⓑ The traffic was loud. The neighbors were loud, but I couldn't sleep.

 Ⓒ The traffic and the neighbors were loud, so I couldn't sleep.

 Ⓓ The traffic was loud and so were the neighbors; but I couldn't sleep.

Writing

Many tests will ask you to respond to a writing prompt. A writing prompt is a question or statement that you are asked to respond to.

> Why is George Washington often called "The Father of Our Country"? Explain your answer.

The following is a list of guidelines to use when responding to a writing prompt.

Read the Prompt
- Read the instructions carefully. Sometimes you will be given a choice of questions or topics to write about. You don't want to respond to more questions than you need to.
- Remember, there is no one right response to a writing prompt; there are only stronger and weaker arguments.

Prewrite
- Before you write your answer, jot down some details to include.
- You may find it helpful to use a chart, web, illustration, or outline to help you organize the information you want to include in your response.
- Even if you aren't asked to, it is always a good idea to include facts and examples that support your answer. If the prompt asks you to respond to a reading passage, you can include specific examples from the passage to strengthen your argument.

Draft
- Begin your answer with a **topic sentence** that answers the main question and gives the main idea.
- Write **supporting sentences** that give details and tell more about your main idea. All of these sentences should relate to the topic sentence.
- If you are allowed, skip lines as you write. That way you'll have space to correct your mistakes once you're done writing.

Proofread
- Make sure to proofread your draft for missing words, grammar, punctuation, capitalization, indentation, and spelling. Correct your mistakes.

Testing It Out
Now read the following topic sentence that is the beginning of a response to the sample prompt. It has been formatted correctly, beginning with an indentation. All spelling and grammar mistakes have been corrected.

> I think that George Washington is called "The Father of Our Country" because he played such an important role in the American Revolution and he was our first President. He was the general of the colonial army when it fought against the British, and if it hadn't been for his good leadership the colonies might not have won the war.

Writing Practice

Directions: Write a two- or three-paragraph response to one of the questions below.

- **A role model is a person that you can look up to and learn from. Who is your role model? Why?**

- **Why is it important to protect our environment? What are some things we can all do to help?**

_____

_____

_____

_____

_____

_____

_____

_____

_____

_____

_____

_____

_____

_____

_____

_____

Math: Draw a Diagram

Many standardized tests will ask you to solve math story, or word, problems. Use the following strategies to help solve story problems quickly. Remember, though, not every strategy can be used with every story problem. You will have to choose the best strategy.

Sometimes it's helpful to draw a diagram to visualize the activity described in a story problem. Diagrams can help you understand a problem and figure out the answer. When you draw a tree diagram, all the possible outcomes of an event are shown. You can then find the correct answer.

EXAMPLE

There are two targets at the arcade. What are all of the possible outcomes if Jeremy tosses one ball at each of the two targets?

Ⓐ yellow 1, red 1, blue 1

Ⓑ yellow 1, yellow 2, red 1,
     red 2, blue 1, blue 2

Ⓒ yellow 2, red 2, blue 2

Ⓓ yellow 2, red 1, blue 2, red 2

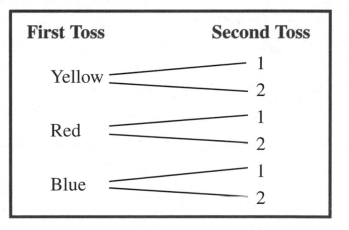

- Start your tree diagram with the first target. List all your possible outcomes for hitting that target. Then draw branches to show all of the possible outcomes for hitting the second target.

- There are 6 possible outcomes for the game: yellow 1, yellow 2, red 1, red 2, blue 1, blue 2. The answer is **B**.

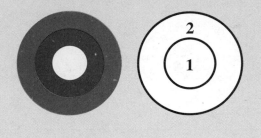

When you draw a tree diagram, do the following:

❑ Read the problem carefully.

❑ Determine what information you need to solve the problem.

❑ Decide how to draw a tree diagram to organize the possible outcomes.

❑ Draw a tree diagram based on the information in the problem.

❑ Solve the problem.

Diagram Practice

Directions: Draw a tree diagram in the space provided to help you solve each problem.

1 **What are the possible outcomes of tossing a penny and then a nickel?**

- Ⓐ heads heads, heads tails, tails heads, tails tails
- Ⓑ heads tails, heads heads, tails tails
- Ⓒ tails heads, heads tails
- Ⓓ tails heads, tails tails

2 **Grant went to get a frozen yogurt from the concession stand. He could choose vanilla, chocolate, or twist yogurt. He could have a cup, wafer cone, or sugar cone. How many possible combinations does Grant have?**

- Ⓕ 6 combinations
- Ⓖ 3 combinations
- Ⓗ 8 combinations
- Ⓙ 9 combinations

Math: Trick Questions

Sometimes you're given trick questions on tests. You may be able to solve a trick question but the answer is not one of the choices given. In this case, you fill in "None of these."

EXAMPLE

There were 488 balloons decorating the gymnasium for a party. There were 97 students at the party. If each student brought home an equal number of balloons after the party, how many balloons were left over?

Ⓐ   2 balloons   Ⓒ   12 balloons

Ⓑ   46 balloons   Ⓓ   None of these

• First, determine what you need to do to solve the problem. Since you have to know the number of balloons left over, you need to find a remainder from a division problem.

• The correct answer is not one of your answer choices. Check your work and then fill in D, the "None of these" choice.

$$\begin{array}{r} 5\,R3 \\ 97\overline{)488} \\ -\underline{485} \\ 3 \end{array}$$

When you have to solve questions for which the answer may not be given:

❑   Read the problem carefully.

❑   Determine what information you need to solve the problem.

❑   Solve the problem.

❑   Check for the correct answer.

❑   Review your work for accuracy and then mark "None of these."

Trick Questions Practice

Directions: Solve each problem. Then circle your answer.
If the correct answer is not given, write it on the line provided.

1 The school basketball team scored a total of 1,148 points during 28 games in the season. What was the average number of points scored per game?

Correct Answer: _____

Ⓐ 47 points   Ⓒ 40 points

Ⓑ 1,120 points   Ⓓ None of these

2 Wendy was trying to figure out the area of her desk. The length is 25 inches and the width is 48 inches. What is the area of Wendy's desk?

Correct Answer: _____

Ⓕ 1,200 square inches

Ⓖ 1,125 square inches

Ⓗ 73 square inches

Ⓙ None of these

3 Scott ran 1 mile in 7 minutes and 42 seconds at the start of the track season. By the end of the track season, Scott could run 1 mile in 6 minutes and 37 seconds. How much time did Scott cut off his running time?

Correct Answer: _____

Ⓐ 1 minute, 3 seconds

Ⓑ 1 minute, 9 seconds

Ⓒ 5 seconds

Ⓓ None of these

4 If each 😊 stands for 3 people, how would you show 12 people?

Correct Answer: _____

Ⓕ 😊 😊

Ⓖ 😊 😊 😊 😊

Ⓗ 😊 😊 😊 😊 😊

Ⓙ None of these

Math: Paper and Pencil

It often helps to work through problems using paper and pencil. It allows you to see and check the work you have done. Some test questions do not give multiple choice answers. You will need to use paper and pencil when you have to find answers to these questions.

EXAMPLE **There are 32 cartons of yo-yos. Each carton has 145 yo-yos. They are ready to be shipped to several stores in a truck. How many yo-yos in total are being shipped on the truck?**

- Since you do not have any answers to choose from, you have to figure out the answer to the question using paper and pencil.

```
   145
 x  32
   290
   435
4,640 yo-yos
```

- Use paper and pencil to multiply 145 x 32. This is the total number of yo-yos on the truck.
- Then, use paper and pencil again to check the answer you found the first time. When checking multiplication, you change the order of the factors.
- You know the answer is 4,640 yo-yos.

```
    32
 x 145
   160
   128
    32
4,640 yo-yos
```

When you use pencil and paper, do the following:
- ❑ Read the problem carefully.
- ❑ Write neatly so that you do not make errors.
- ❑ Solve the problem.
- ❑ Check your work.

Paper and Pencil Practice

Directions: Solve each problem using paper and pencil. Do your work in the space provided.

1 If you burn 318 calories in 60 minutes of playing tennis, how many calories would you burn in 30 minutes? _____

2 A chicken pot pie was cut into 8 slices. For dinner, the Wilsons ate $\frac{3}{8}$ of the pie. For lunch, the Wilsons ate $\frac{1}{4}$ of the pie. How much of the pie was eaten? _____

3 What is the area of the triangle?

_____

4 ft.

← 3 ft. →

4 A roller coaster holds a total of 184 people. If each car holds 8 people, how many cars are there?

_____

5 Jesse bought a pack of cards for $1.25 and a baseball for $8.39. He has $5.36 left over. How much money did he start with?

_____

6 A box of 20 tennis balls costs $35.80. What is the cost for each tennis ball?_____

Math: Guess and Check

One way to solve problems on tests is to use Guess and Check. You make a guess based on the information in the problem. Then you check it and revise your guess until you find the correct answer to the problem.

EXAMPLE

The sum of two numbers is 21 and their product is 98. What are the 2 numbers?

Ⓐ 12 and 8   Ⓒ 77 and 21

Ⓑ 14 and 7   Ⓓ 7 and 9

• When you guess and check you need to try a set of numbers to see how close you get to the sum 21 and the product 98.
Guess: 12 and 8

12 + 8 = 20
12 × 8 = 96
Check: 20 < 21 and 96 < 98

• Since your numbers were small, you should try larger numbers.
Guess: 14 and 7

14 + 7 = 21
14 × 7 = 98
Check: 21=21   and 98=98

• Your guess is correct. The sum of 14 and 7 is 21 and the product of 14 and 7 is 98. The correct answer is **B.**

When you use guess and check, do the following:

❑ Read the problem carefully.

❑ Make a reasonable first guess.

❑ Revise your guess based on whether your answer was too high or low.

❑ Be sure your answer is reasonable based on the question.

Guess and Check Practice

Directions: Guess and check to find the correct answer.

1 Giraffes and birds are drinking at a watering hole. There are 10 animals with a total of 30 legs there. How many 2-legged birds are there? How many 4-legged giraffes are there?

Ⓐ 5 birds, 5 giraffes

Ⓑ 4 birds, 3 giraffes

Ⓒ 2 birds, 5 giraffes

Ⓓ 6 birds, 1 giraffe

2 There are two numbers whose product is 98 and quotient is 2. What are the two numbers?

Ⓕ 49, 8   Ⓗ 14, 7

Ⓖ 14, 2   Ⓙ 96, 2

3 Tyson spent $16.09 at the store. What 2 items did he buy?

Ⓐ model airplane and robot

Ⓑ model airplane and race car

Ⓒ robot and race car

Ⓓ None of these

4 You have 5 coins that total $0.71. What coins do you have?

Ⓕ 3 dimes, 1 nickel, 1 penny

Ⓖ 1 quarter, 3 dimes, 1 penny

Ⓗ 2 quarters, 1 dime, 1 nickel, 1 penny

Ⓙ 2 quarters, 2 dimes, 1 penny

Math: Estimation

On multiple choice tests you can estimate the answer as a way to eliminate some of the choices.

EXAMPLE

A sailboat takes 124 passengers on a cruise on a lake. If the sailboat makes 53 tours a month, how many people ride on the boat?

Ⓐ 5,789

Ⓒ 6,845 people

Ⓑ 5,499

Ⓓ 6,572 people

- First, estimate the answer by rounding. You should round to the most precise place needed for the problem. In this case, round to the nearest ten.

        124 rounds to 120
        53 rounds to 50
        120 x 50 = 6,000

- You can cross off choices A and B since they have a 5 rather than a 6 in the thousands place.
- Find the exact answer by multiplying:

$$\begin{array}{r} 124 \\ \times\ \ 53 \\ \hline 372 \\ 620 \\ \hline 6,572 \end{array}$$

- There would be 6,572 riders. The correct answer is **D**.

When you estimate, do the following:

❑ Read the problem carefully.

❑ Round the numbers you need.

❑ Estimate the answer.

❑ Cross off any answers that are not close to your estimate.

❑ Find the exact answer.

Estimation Practice

Directions: Solve these problems using estimation.

1 A truck driver makes 23 trips each month. Each trip is 576 miles long. How many miles does the truck driver travel in a month?

Ⓐ 13,248 miles Ⓒ 13,589 miles

Ⓑ 12,248 miles Ⓓ 14,553 miles

2 Terrance collected 468 seashells in 18 visits to the beach. How many seashells did he collect during each visit?

Ⓕ 29 Ⓗ 32

Ⓖ 26 Ⓙ 23

3 1,234 ÷ 22 =

Ⓐ 61 R8 Ⓒ 57 R7

Ⓑ 63 R1 Ⓓ 56 R2

4 The area of a rectangle is 943 square inches. The length of the rectangle is 41 inches. What is the width of the rectangle?

Ⓕ 24 inches Ⓗ 23 inches

Ⓖ 32 inches Ⓙ 18 inches

?

41 inches

5 4,098 – 1,209 =

Ⓐ 2,989 Ⓒ 2,643

Ⓑ 2,889 Ⓓ 2,612

6 There are 21 fish in every square foot of water in a lake. If the lake is 812 square feet, how many fish are in the lake?

Ⓕ 17,052 Ⓗ 29,987

Ⓖ 23,708 Ⓙ 14,879

Math: Incomplete Information

One of the answer choices for some problems on tests may be "Not enough information." In this case, you may not be given all of the information you need to solve the problem. If you determine that you cannot solve the problem with the information given, you fill in the "Not enough information" choice.

EXAMPLE

There are 62 students on a class trip. They are taking a bus to the nature park. The ride to the park takes 25 minutes and the ride home takes 30 minutes. Lunch at the park costs $3.25 per child. How much money do the students spend to get into the park?

Ⓐ $201.50   Ⓒ $120.25

Ⓑ $50.00   Ⓓ   Not enough information

- Read the problem to find out the question you need to answer.
  How much does it cost to get into the nature park?
- Determine what information you have.
  How many students went to the park
  How long it took to travel to the park and back
  How much lunch costs
- You do not have enough information to answer the question since you do not know the entrance fee to get into the nature park.

- Reread the problem to verify that you do not have enough information to solve the problem.
- You do not have enough information in this case, so your answer is **D.**

When you think you have incomplete information, do the following:
- ❑   Read the problem carefully.
- ❑   Determine what information you need to solve the problem.
- ❑   Check to see if you have all the information to solve the problem.
- ❑   Make sure the information you need to solve the problem is missing.

Incomplete Information Practice

Directions: Find the correct answer to the following questions.

1 Dylan drew a shape with 4 sides. Two sides were the same length and one corner was 90 degrees. What shape did Dylan draw?

Ⓐ square   Ⓒ triangle

Ⓑ rectangle   Ⓓ Not enough information

2 Aijuin used $\frac{1}{8}$ of a stick of butter to make muffins. She then used $\frac{2}{3}$ of a cup of flour to make bread. How much butter did she use in the muffins and bread?

Ⓕ $\frac{1}{8}$ stick   Ⓗ $\frac{2}{3}$ stick

Ⓖ 1.4 stick   Ⓙ Not enough information

3 A store manager ordered 4 cases of juice boxes. There are 6 boxes in each package and 12 packages in a case. How many juice boxes did he order altogether?

Ⓐ 24 boxes   Ⓒ 48 boxes

Ⓑ 288 boxes   Ⓓ Not enough information

4 Lydia went to school at 8:00 in the morning. She had soccer practice after school for $1\frac{1}{2}$ hours. What time did Lydia get home in the evening?

Ⓕ 5:30   Ⓗ 4:00

Ⓖ 9:30   Ⓙ Not enough information

5 Marianne traveled 99.5 miles in one weekend. If she traveled 46.9 miles on Saturday, how far did she travel on Sunday?

Ⓐ 52.6 miles   Ⓒ 34 miles

Ⓑ 146.4 miles   Ⓓ Not enough information

Math: Use a Calculator

You may be allowed to use a calculator with some standardized tests. Using a calculator can save you time, especially when you need to compute multi-digit numbers. A calculator also allows you to quickly check your work.

EXAMPLE   **A store has 3,802 compact discs on the shelves. The store receives 2 new cases of compact discs. There are 320 compact discs in each case. How many compact discs does the store have now?**

Ⓐ   640 compact discs   Ⓒ   4,442 compact discs

Ⓑ   3,802 compact discs   Ⓓ   3,482 compact discs

- To solve the problem, you need to multiply a two digit number by a one digit number and then add the product to a four digit number. It is quicker and easier to use a calculator, especially on a timed test.

320	3,802
x 2	+ 640
640	4,442

- The store has 4,442 compact discs. The correct answer is **C.**
- When you use a calculator you can make a complex problem easier. However, you must be sure to key in the correct numbers to find the right answer.

When you use a calculator, do the following:

- ❑   Read the problem carefully.
- ❑   Be sure to key in the correct numbers.
- ❑   Solve the problem.

Calculator Practice

Directions: Find the correct answer using a calculator.

1 Rita and Miguel make a $1,268 profit by walking dogs. They share their profit equally. How much money does Miguel make?

Ⓐ $634.00   Ⓒ $420.30

Ⓑ $1,268.00   Ⓓ $256.89

2 There are 2,390 bees in the bee exhibit at the zoo. If 1,289 bees are moved to a new area, how many remain in the original exhibit?

Ⓕ 1,598 bees   Ⓗ 1,101 bees

Ⓖ 1,504 bees   Ⓙ 1,203 bees

3 At the first performance of a play there were 976 people in the audience. On the second night there were 1,298 people in the audience. On the third night there were 1,145 people in the audience. What is the total number of people who attended the show?

Ⓐ 1,897 people   Ⓒ 2,274 people

Ⓑ 2,867 people   Ⓓ 3,419 people

TICKETS $4.25

4 The school play sold out every night. The play ran for 3 nights and each night 345 people attended. How much money did the school play make?

Ⓕ $1,239.50   Ⓗ $1,035.00

Ⓖ $1,466.25   Ⓙ $4,398.75

5 David scored 1,832 points on a video game. Susan scored 2 times more than David. Paul scored 234 points less than Susan. What was Paul's score?

Ⓐ 3,320 points   Ⓒ 3,430 points

Ⓑ 3,664 points   Ⓓ 468 points

SCORE: 1,832

Math: Computation

Most standardized tests contain math sections where you must solve a variety of number equations. These questions test your ability to find exact answers to math problems. You will often be allowed to use scrap paper to work out these problems, but the work you show on scrap paper will not count.

Here are some tips when solving computation problems:

- Whenever you are solving a math equation, be sure which operation you must use.
- Even though you will be given answer choices, it's best to work the problem out first using scrap paper. Then you can compare the answer you found to the choices that are given.
- If you have time, double-check your answer to each problem by using the inverse operation. For example, if you add, double-check your answer by subtracting.

- Keep in mind that an equation may be written on one line, or it may be stacked. Even though these problems look different, they are the same problem.

$$995 + 226 = ? \qquad \begin{array}{r} 995 \\ +226 \\ \hline ? \end{array}$$

Other Things to Keep in Mind

- When solving problems involving decimals, make sure your answer choice shows the decimal point in the correct place.
- If your problem contains units (such as 2 centimeters + 50 millimeters = X millimeters), be sure that you find the answer choice with the correct units labeled. Many tests will try to confuse you by substituting one unit for another.
- Finally, if you get to a tough problem, look carefully at the answer choices and use logic to decide which one makes the most sense. Then plug this choice into the equation and see if it works.

Computation Practice

Directions: Find the answer to each problem below.

1 **5989 + 2697 =**

ⓐ 3292

ⓑ 8668

ⓒ 8686

ⓓ None of the above

2 $\frac{8}{9} + \frac{5}{9} + \frac{1}{9} =$

ⓕ $\frac{5}{9}$

ⓖ $1\frac{5}{9}$

ⓗ $1\frac{3}{9}$

ⓙ $\frac{9}{15}$

3 **6.211 + 9.938 =**

ⓐ 16.049

ⓑ 16.149

ⓒ 161.49

ⓓ 160.149

4 **$26.16 ÷ 8 =**

ⓕ $3.207

ⓖ $3.27

ⓗ $3.37

ⓙ $33.37

5 $\frac{18}{15} - \frac{9}{15} =$

ⓐ $\frac{9}{15}$

ⓑ $\frac{15}{9}$

ⓒ $\frac{13}{15}$

ⓓ $\frac{17}{15}$

6 **5,951 + 3,291 =**

ⓕ 9,242

ⓖ 929.4

ⓗ 924.4

ⓙ 892.2

7 **18.2 – 9.53 =**

ⓐ 86.7

ⓑ 8.76

ⓒ 8.7

ⓓ 8.67

8 $\frac{4}{5} + \frac{4}{5} =$

ⓕ $\frac{5}{8}$

ⓖ $1\frac{3}{5}$

ⓗ 5

ⓙ 13

Math: Concepts

Standardized tests also test your understanding of important math concepts you will have learned about in school.

The following is a list of concepts that you may be tested on when you take a standardized test with math problems.

Number Concepts

You may have to show that you understand the following number concepts:

- recognizing the standard and metric units of measure used for weighing and finding length and distance.
- equivalent measures (how many feet in a yard, etc.).
- recognizing place value (the ones, tens, hundreds, and thousands places; the tenths and hundredths places).
- telling time to the minute.
- using a calendar.
- reading a thermometer.
- rounding up and down to the nearest five, ten, or hundred.
- fraction/decimal equivalents.
- reading/writing numbers in expanded notation.

Geometry

It's also common to see questions about geometry on standardized tests. You may be asked to:

- identify solid shapes such as prisms, spheres, cubes, cylinders, and cones.
- calculate the perimeter and area of flat shapes.

- find the line of symmetry in a flat shape.
- tell about the number of angles and sides of flat shapes.
- recognize parallel and perpendicular lines.
- recognize congruent shapes.

Other Things to Keep in Mind

The best way to prepare for concept questions is **to study math words and definitions in advance**. However, if you come to a difficult problem, think of what you know about the topic and **eliminate answer choices that don't make sense**. For example, if you are asked to identify a shape that you don't recognize, you may recognize some of other shapes mentioned and know that they couldn't be correct. Use the process of elimination whenever you come to a tough question.

Concepts Practice

Directions: Find the answer to each problem below.

1 3 yards = X inches
X = ?

Ⓐ 24

Ⓑ 32

Ⓒ 36

Ⓓ None of the above

2 Which of the following numbers has a 5 in the hundredths place?

Ⓕ 505.21

Ⓖ 251.32

Ⓗ 31.335

Ⓙ 63.251

3 What time does this clock show?

Ⓐ 8:52

Ⓑ 9:52

Ⓒ 10:52

Ⓓ None of the above

4 What is the number 547 rounded to the nearest hundred?

Ⓕ 550

Ⓖ 560

Ⓗ 500

Ⓙ 600

5 ¼ is equal to which of the following?

Ⓐ .04

Ⓑ .40

Ⓒ .25

Ⓓ .50

6 Which of the following letters has a line of symmetry?

Ⓕ R

Ⓖ W

Ⓗ Z

Ⓙ S

7 How many feet are there in one mile?

Ⓐ 5,028

Ⓑ 5,280

Ⓒ 5,820

Ⓓ 8,520

8 What kind of lines are shown here?

Ⓕ right

Ⓖ parallel

Ⓗ perpendicular

Ⓙ obtuse

Math: Applications

You will often be asked to apply what you know about math to a new type of problem or set of information. Even if you aren't exactly sure how to solve a problem of this type, you can usually draw on what you already know to make the most logical choice.

When preparing for standardized tests, you may want to practice some of the following:

- how to use a number line with whole numbers and decimals.
- putting numbers in order from least to greatest and using greater than/less than symbols.
- recognizing basic number patterns and object patterns and extending them.
- writing an equation to solve a problem.
- reading bar graphs, tally charts, or pictographs.
- reading pie charts.
- reading simple line graphs.
- reading and making Venn diagrams.

Other Things to Keep in Mind

When answering application questions, be sure to **read each problem carefully**. You may want to **use scrap paper to help you work out some problems**.

Again, if you come to a problem you aren't sure how to solve or a word/idea you don't recognize, try to **eliminate answer choices** by using what you do know. Then go back and check your answer choice in the context of the problem.

Applications Practice

Directions: Find the answer to each problem below.

1 Which number could be put in the empty box to make this statement true? $\frac{8}{7} > \square$

Ⓐ $\frac{7}{8}$

Ⓑ 7

Ⓒ 8

Ⓓ 8.7

2 Which number comes next in this pattern? 5, 15, 45, _____

Ⓕ 50

Ⓖ 60

Ⓗ 135

Ⓙ None of the above

3 What equation would you use to find out the number of minutes in one week?

Ⓐ 24 x 60

Ⓑ 7 x 24 x 60

Ⓒ 7 x 24 x 365

Ⓓ 365 ÷ 60

4 Which symbol fits in the empty box? $3 \times \frac{1}{3} \square 5 \times \frac{1}{5}$

Ⓕ < Ⓗ =

Ⓖ > Ⓙ None of the above

5 Which type of graph would be best to show how the average weekly temperature changed in one town from month to month?

Ⓐ a pie chart

Ⓑ a tally chart

Ⓒ a bar graph

Ⓓ a line graph

6 If you wanted to compare the features of two different solid shapes, the best thing to use would be a

Ⓕ Venn diagram.

Ⓖ pie chart.

Ⓗ tally chart.

Ⓙ line graph.

7 What letter is missing from this pattern? CDE _____ GCDEFG

Ⓐ C

Ⓑ A

Ⓒ G

Ⓓ F

Social Studies

Standardized tests often include questions about social studies topics. You may see questions about maps, geography, history, and government.

The following is a list of topics that may be covered on the test and tips to use when solving the questions. Sample questions are also included.

Map Skills

You will probably be asked to look at a map and answer questions about it. Keep these tips in mind:

- All maps include the following elements: a **compass rose**, a **legend** with symbols, and a **scale**.
- Globes and maps often show a **grid** of lines that can be used to locate specific points.
- Lines of **latitude** are horizontal, and lines of **longitude** are vertical. Both lines are measured in **degrees**.
- Maps are used for different purposes. **Political maps** show boundaries made by governments, while **topographical maps** show different landforms. **Population maps** show the populations of different areas.

When you read a map, be sure to read the title first. Make sure you understand the kind of information the map is presenting.

Geography

Geography is the study of the land and its features. Make a quick review of these geography terms:

- **natural features:** plateau, mountain, ocean, bay, peninsula, island, isthmus, coastline
- **other geography terms:** hemisphere, equator, prime meridian, continent, country, state, capital

Social Studies

Time Lines

A time line organizes historical events in the order in which they occurred. It is a helpful picture that can help you figure out which events happened first and which happened later on. Some questions will ask you to use a time line to answer a question:

EXAMPLE

Where on the time line would you place the 1958 founding of NASA?

Ⓐ before 1

Ⓒ between 2 and 3

Ⓑ between 1 and 2

Ⓓ between 3 and 4

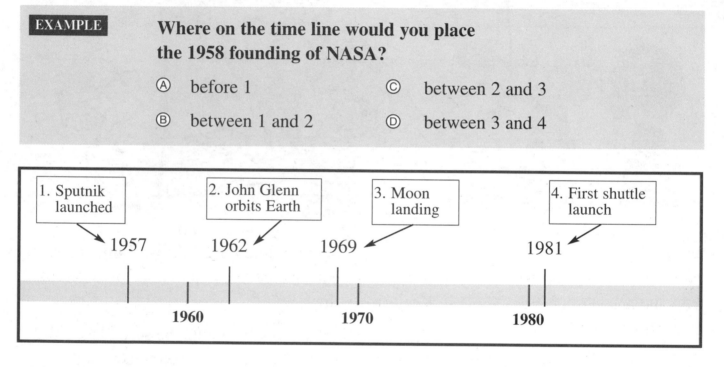

1. Sputnik launched — 1957

2. John Glenn orbits Earth — 1962

3. Moon landing — 1969

4. First shuttle launch — 1981

1960   1970   1980

• The correct answer is **B** because the 1958 event occurred after the 1957 Sputnik launch, but before John Glenn's Earth orbit in 1962.

Social Studies

Reading Passages

You will probably be asked to read a passage about a social studies topic and to answer questions about it. An excellent strategy is to read the questions before you read the passage, so that you know what to look for. Keep in mind that these questions will often ask you to think about:

- the writer's point of view
- the kind of source (encyclopedia entry, diary entry, letter)
- the possible causes or results of the events described in the passage

Research Skills

Some questions will test your ability to think like a historian. You will be asked about different sources that historians use to find out historical data.

Social Studies Knowledge

Some social studies questions will ask specific questions about topics you have been studying in class, such as:

- the Constitution, the Bill of Rights, and the Declaration of Independence
- the branches of government (executive, legislative, judicial)
- levels of government (local, state, federal)
- immigration
- explorers

As you answer these questions, be sure to make sure you understand what the question is asking. Get rid of the unreasonable answers first, and then make your best guess.

Social Studies Practice

Directions: For questions 1–5, find the correct answer.

1 The line of longitude at 0 degrees is called the

Ⓐ equator.

Ⓑ prime meridian.

Ⓒ continental divide.

Ⓓ Greenwich mean time.

2 Which document was written first?

Ⓕ Emancipation Proclamation

Ⓖ Bill of Rights

Ⓗ Constitution

Ⓙ Declaration of Independence

3 At which level of government does the President work?

Ⓐ local

Ⓑ county

Ⓒ state

Ⓓ federal

4 Which president bought the land called the Louisiana Purchase?

Ⓕ George Washington

Ⓖ Thomas Jefferson

Ⓗ Abraham Lincoln

Ⓙ Woodrow Wilson

5 What was the name of the ship that brought the Pilgrims to America?

Ⓐ Pinta

Ⓑ New Orleans

Ⓒ Half Moon

Ⓓ Mayflower

Social Studies Practice

Directions: For questions 6 and 7, read the passage and answer the questions that follow.

The best thing that ever happened to Los Angeles was when William Mulholland brought water to the city! In 1913, he arranged for the Los Angeles Aqueduct to bring thousands of gallons of water from the Owens River Valley, over 238 miles away. Now people could have farms, feed animals, and grow beautiful gardens. More people built businesses, and more people moved in. Our population increased dramatically as a result of that water from the Owens Valley. If it weren't for Mr. Mulholland, my city wouldn't be what it is today.

6 **The person who wrote this essay probably lives in**

Ⓕ The Owens Valley.

Ⓖ Los Angeles.

Ⓗ Washington, D. C.

Ⓙ Seattle, Washington.

7 **What could be another result of diverting the water from the Owens Valley?**

Ⓐ The oceans would rise.

Ⓑ Los Angeles would get more rain.

Ⓒ Crops in the Owens Valley wouldn't grow.

Ⓓ There would be more fish in the river.

Science

You will often see science questions on standardized tests. These questions may be about scientific facts. They may also test your ability to "think like a scientist." This means you must use data (information) to make predictions and draw conclusions.

The following list of tips this page and the next includes some words you will need to know. It also contains examples of the types of science questions you may see on a test.

Science Words

Many science questions will include at least one of the words below:

- **research question:** the question that a scientist asks
  (*How does sunlight affect plants?*)
- **hypothesis:** a scientist's possible answer to the question
  (*If there is not enough sunlight, the plants will not grow.*)
- **experiment:** a test to see if the hypothesis is correct.

- **prediction:** a guess about the future results of an experiment
  (*The plants with more sunlight will be taller than the plants with less sunlight.*)
- **observation:** when a scientist watches the results of an experiment
- **data:** the information collected in an experiment
  (*The plant grew 3 inches this month.*)
- **conclusion:** a statement based on information gathered in an experiment
  (*Sunlight helps plants to grow.*)

Science

Science Processes

Some science questions ask you to think about the scientific process and answer questions about data or experiments. Keep in mind the steps of a scientific experiment and use common sense as you look at your choices.

EXAMPLE

A scientist wants to find out if milk evaporates faster than water. Which experiment would give the best results?

Ⓐ Put equal amounts of milk and water into two different bowls and leave them in a dry area.

Ⓑ Combine milk and water into one bowl and leave it in a dry area.

Ⓒ Put a small amount of water in one bowl and a greater amount of milk in another bowl and leave them in a dry area.

Ⓓ Put three containers of water in three different areas. Add milk each day.

The correct answer would be **A** because the scientist should use identical amounts of milk and water in different containers to measure which liquid is evaporating faster.

Science Knowledge

Science questions on your standardized test may require you to know specific scientific information. This may include information about:

- types of rocks and minerals
- electricity and magnetism
- our solar system
- properties of matter
- the behavior of living things

EXAMPLE

Which animal is not a mammal?

Ⓐ chickadee   Ⓒ badger

Ⓑ wildebeest   Ⓓ mule deer

In this example, you can easily eliminate **C** and **D,** because badgers and mule deer are both mammals. Even though you may not know what a wildebeest is, you know you can select **A** as the correct answer, because a chickadee is a bird, birds lays eggs–and a mammal does not lay eggs.

Science Practice

Directions: Read the passage and answer the questions that follow.

The Earth is a restless place. Although it may seem perfectly solid to you, the earth below your feet is moving at this very moment! The continents rest on top of the brittle crust of the Earth, which has broken apart into pieces. These pieces, called *tectonic plates*, float around on top of the molten interior of the Earth, much like crackers floating in a bowl of soup. Molten rock continues to push up through cracks in the plates, pushing the plates even further apart. Over 200 million years ago, the continents were connected together as one piece of land. Over the years, they have split off and drifted further and further apart, at the rate of about 1 inch every year.

1 **According to this passage, why do tectonic plates move around?**

   Ⓐ They are floating on water.

   Ⓑ Molten rock pushes up through the cracks and pushes them apart.

   Ⓒ The continents are trying to connect together again.

   Ⓓ The crust of the Earth is breaking.

2 **According to this passage, about how long would it take for Europe and North America to move one foot further apart?**

   Ⓕ 6 years

   Ⓖ 8 years

   Ⓗ 10 years

   Ⓙ 12 years

3 **What piece of evidence would help scientists to prove that the continents used to be connected?**

   Ⓐ Similar fossils on the coasts of two different continents.

   Ⓑ A photograph of the two continents connected.

   Ⓒ Measuring the temperature of the oceans.

   Ⓓ Timing how long it takes for a continent to move one inch.

Practice Test and Final Test Information

The remainder of this book is made up of two tests. On page 79, you will find a Practice Test. On page 125, you will find a Final Test. These tests will give you a chance to put the tips you have learned to work. There is also a name and answer sheet preceding each test and an answer key at the end of the book.

Here are some things to remember as you take these tests:

• Be sure you understand all the directions before you begin each test.

• Ask an adult questions about the directions if you do not understand them.

• Work as quickly as you can during each test. There are no time limits on the Practice Test, but you should try to make good use of your time. There are suggested time limits on the Final Test to give you practice managing your time.

• You will notice little GO and STOP signs at the bottom of the test pages. When you see a GO sign, continue on to the next page if you feel ready. The STOP sign means you are at the end of a section. When you see a STOP sign, take a break.

• When you change an answer, be sure to erase your first mark completely.

• You can guess at an answer or skip difficult items and go back to them later.

• Use the tips you have learned whenever you can.

• It is OK to be a little nervous. You may even do better.

• After you have completed your tests, check your answers with the answer key. You can record the number of questions you got correct for each unit on the recording sheet on page 76.

• When you complete all the lessons in this book, you will be on your way to test success!

Table of Contents

Name Sheet

Fill in **only one** letter for each item. If you change an answer, make sure to erase your first mark completely. This is a practice name sheet like the ones you will use in school. Follow these directions:

1. Use a No. 2 pencil.

2. Write your name in the boxes. Put only one letter in each box. Then fill in one little circle below each letter that has that letter of your name.

3. Fill in all the other information.

STUDENT'S NAME			SCHOOL
LAST	FIRST	MI	TEACHER

FEMALE ○   MALE ○

BIRTHDATE

MONTH	DAY	YEAR
JAN ○	⓪ ⓪	⓪
FEB ○	① ①	①
MAR ○	② ②	②
APR ○	③ ③	③
MAY ○	④	④
JUN ○	⑤ ⑤	⑤
JUL ○	⑥ ⑥	⑥
AUG ○	⑦ ⑦	⑦
SEP ○	⑧ ⑧	⑧
OCT ○	⑨ ⑨	⑨
NOV ○		
DEC ○		

GRADE

④   ⑤   ⑥   ⑦   ⑧

Name bubble columns: A B C D E F G H I J K L M N O P Q R S T U V W X Y Z

Record Your Scores

After you have completed and checked each test, record your scores below. Do not count your answers for the sample questions or the writing pages.

Practice Test

Unit 1 Reading
Number of Questions: 34   Number Correct _____

Unit 2 Language Arts
Number of Questions: 43   Number Correct _____

Unit 3 Mathematics
Number of Questions: 31   Number Correct _____

Unit 4 Social Studies
Number of Questions: 16   Number Correct _____

Unit 5 Science
Number of Questions: 18   Number Correct _____

Final Test

Unit 1 Reading
Number of Questions: 39   Number Correct _____

Unit 2 Language Arts
Number of Questions: 51   Number Correct _____

Unit 3 Mathcmatics
Number of Questions: 48   Number Correct _____

Unit 4 Social Studies
Number of Questions: 7   Number Correct _____

Unit 5 Science
Number of Questions: 10   Number Correct _____

Practice Test Answer Sheet

Fill in **only one** letter for each item. If you change an answer, make sure to erase your first mark completely.

Unit 1: Reading, pages 79-93

A Ⓐ Ⓑ Ⓒ Ⓓ	**7** Ⓐ Ⓑ Ⓒ Ⓓ	**15** Ⓐ Ⓑ Ⓒ Ⓓ	**22** Ⓐ Ⓑ Ⓒ Ⓓ	**29** Ⓕ Ⓖ Ⓗ Ⓙ
B Ⓕ Ⓖ Ⓗ Ⓙ	**8** Ⓕ Ⓖ Ⓗ Ⓙ	**16** Ⓕ Ⓖ Ⓗ Ⓙ	**23** Ⓕ Ⓖ Ⓗ Ⓙ	**30** Ⓐ Ⓑ Ⓒ Ⓓ
1 Ⓐ Ⓑ Ⓒ Ⓓ	**9** Ⓐ Ⓑ Ⓒ Ⓓ	**17** Ⓐ Ⓑ Ⓒ Ⓓ	**24** Ⓐ Ⓑ Ⓒ Ⓓ	**31** Ⓕ Ⓖ Ⓗ Ⓙ
2 Ⓕ Ⓖ Ⓗ Ⓙ	**10** Ⓕ Ⓖ Ⓗ Ⓙ	**18** Ⓕ Ⓖ Ⓗ Ⓙ	**25** Ⓕ Ⓖ Ⓗ Ⓙ	**32** Ⓐ Ⓑ Ⓒ Ⓓ
3 Ⓐ Ⓑ Ⓒ Ⓓ	**11** Ⓐ Ⓑ Ⓒ Ⓓ	**19** Ⓐ Ⓑ Ⓒ Ⓓ	**26** Ⓐ Ⓑ Ⓒ Ⓓ	**33** Ⓕ Ⓖ Ⓗ Ⓙ
4 Ⓕ Ⓖ Ⓗ Ⓙ	**12** Ⓕ Ⓖ Ⓗ Ⓙ	**20** Ⓕ Ⓖ Ⓗ Ⓙ	**27** Ⓕ Ⓖ Ⓗ Ⓙ	**34** Ⓐ Ⓑ Ⓒ Ⓓ
5 Ⓐ Ⓑ Ⓒ Ⓓ	**13** Ⓐ Ⓑ Ⓒ Ⓓ	**21** Ⓐ Ⓑ Ⓒ Ⓓ	**D** Ⓐ Ⓑ Ⓒ Ⓓ	
6 Ⓕ Ⓖ Ⓗ Ⓙ	**14** Ⓕ Ⓖ Ⓗ Ⓙ	**C** Ⓐ Ⓑ Ⓒ Ⓓ	**28** Ⓐ Ⓑ Ⓒ Ⓓ	

Unit 2: Language Arts, pages 94-104

A Ⓐ Ⓑ Ⓒ Ⓓ	**9** Ⓐ Ⓑ Ⓒ Ⓓ	**18** Ⓕ Ⓖ Ⓗ Ⓙ Ⓚ	**25** Ⓐ Ⓑ Ⓒ Ⓓ	**34** Ⓕ Ⓖ Ⓗ Ⓙ
1 Ⓐ Ⓑ Ⓒ Ⓓ	**10** Ⓕ Ⓖ Ⓗ Ⓙ	**19** Ⓐ Ⓑ Ⓒ Ⓓ Ⓔ	**26** Ⓕ Ⓖ Ⓗ Ⓙ	**35** Ⓐ Ⓑ Ⓒ Ⓓ
2 Ⓕ Ⓖ Ⓗ Ⓙ	**C** Ⓐ Ⓑ Ⓒ Ⓓ	**20** Ⓕ Ⓖ Ⓗ Ⓙ	**G** Ⓐ Ⓑ Ⓒ Ⓓ Ⓔ	**36** Ⓕ Ⓖ Ⓗ Ⓙ
B Ⓐ Ⓑ Ⓒ Ⓓ	**11** Ⓐ Ⓑ Ⓒ Ⓓ	**D** Ⓐ Ⓑ Ⓒ Ⓓ	**27** Ⓐ Ⓑ Ⓒ Ⓓ	**37** Ⓐ Ⓑ Ⓒ Ⓓ
3 Ⓐ Ⓑ Ⓒ Ⓓ	**12** Ⓕ Ⓖ Ⓗ Ⓙ	**21** Ⓐ Ⓑ Ⓒ Ⓓ	**28** Ⓕ Ⓖ Ⓗ Ⓙ	**38** Ⓕ Ⓖ Ⓗ Ⓙ
4 Ⓕ Ⓖ Ⓗ Ⓙ	**13** Ⓐ Ⓑ Ⓒ Ⓓ	**22** Ⓕ Ⓖ Ⓗ Ⓙ	**29** Ⓐ Ⓑ Ⓒ Ⓓ	**39** Ⓐ Ⓑ Ⓒ Ⓓ
5 Ⓐ Ⓑ Ⓒ Ⓓ	**14** Ⓕ Ⓖ Ⓗ Ⓙ Ⓚ	**E** Ⓐ Ⓑ Ⓒ Ⓓ Ⓔ	**30** Ⓕ Ⓖ Ⓗ Ⓙ	**40** Ⓕ Ⓖ Ⓗ Ⓙ Ⓚ
6 Ⓕ Ⓖ Ⓗ Ⓙ	**15** Ⓐ Ⓑ Ⓒ Ⓓ Ⓔ	**23** Ⓐ Ⓑ Ⓒ Ⓓ Ⓔ	**31** Ⓐ Ⓑ Ⓒ Ⓓ	**41** Ⓐ Ⓑ Ⓒ Ⓓ Ⓔ
7 Ⓐ Ⓑ Ⓒ Ⓓ	**16** Ⓕ Ⓖ Ⓗ Ⓙ Ⓚ	**24** Ⓕ Ⓖ Ⓗ Ⓙ Ⓚ	**32** Ⓕ Ⓖ Ⓗ Ⓙ	**42** Ⓕ Ⓖ Ⓗ Ⓙ Ⓚ
8 Ⓕ Ⓖ Ⓗ Ⓙ	**17** Ⓐ Ⓑ Ⓒ Ⓓ Ⓔ	**F** Ⓐ Ⓑ Ⓒ Ⓓ	**33** Ⓐ Ⓑ Ⓒ Ⓓ	**43** Ⓐ Ⓑ Ⓒ Ⓓ Ⓔ

Unit 3: Mathematics, pages 105-114

A Ⓐ Ⓑ Ⓒ Ⓓ Ⓔ	**6** Ⓕ Ⓖ Ⓗ Ⓙ Ⓚ	**14** Ⓕ Ⓖ Ⓗ Ⓙ	**21** Ⓐ Ⓑ Ⓒ Ⓓ Ⓔ	**28** Ⓐ Ⓑ Ⓒ Ⓓ
B Ⓕ Ⓖ Ⓗ Ⓙ Ⓚ	**7** Ⓐ Ⓑ Ⓒ Ⓓ Ⓔ	**15** Ⓐ Ⓑ Ⓒ Ⓓ	**22** Ⓕ Ⓖ Ⓗ Ⓙ Ⓚ	**29** Ⓕ Ⓖ Ⓗ Ⓙ
1 Ⓐ Ⓑ Ⓒ Ⓓ Ⓔ	**8** Ⓕ Ⓖ Ⓗ Ⓙ Ⓚ	**16** Ⓕ Ⓖ Ⓗ Ⓙ Ⓚ	**23** Ⓐ Ⓑ Ⓒ Ⓓ Ⓔ	**30** Ⓐ Ⓑ Ⓒ Ⓓ
2 Ⓕ Ⓖ Ⓗ Ⓙ Ⓚ	**9** Ⓐ Ⓑ Ⓒ Ⓓ Ⓔ	**17** Ⓐ Ⓑ Ⓒ Ⓓ Ⓔ	**D** Ⓐ Ⓑ Ⓒ Ⓓ	**31** Ⓕ Ⓖ Ⓗ Ⓙ
3 Ⓐ Ⓑ Ⓒ Ⓓ Ⓔ	**10** Ⓕ Ⓖ Ⓗ Ⓙ	**18** Ⓕ Ⓖ Ⓗ Ⓙ Ⓚ	**24** Ⓐ Ⓑ Ⓒ Ⓓ	
4 Ⓕ Ⓖ Ⓗ Ⓙ Ⓚ	**11** Ⓐ Ⓑ Ⓒ Ⓓ	**E** Ⓕ Ⓖ Ⓗ Ⓙ Ⓚ	**25** Ⓕ Ⓖ Ⓗ Ⓙ	
C Ⓐ Ⓑ Ⓒ Ⓓ	**12** Ⓕ Ⓖ Ⓗ Ⓙ	**19** Ⓐ Ⓑ Ⓒ Ⓓ Ⓔ	**26** Ⓐ Ⓑ Ⓒ Ⓓ	
5 Ⓐ Ⓑ Ⓒ Ⓓ	**13** Ⓐ Ⓑ Ⓒ Ⓓ	**20** Ⓕ Ⓖ Ⓗ Ⓙ Ⓚ	**27** Ⓕ Ⓖ Ⓗ Ⓙ	

Practice Test Answer Sheet

Unit 4: Social Studies, pages 115-118

1 Ⓐ Ⓑ Ⓒ Ⓓ   5 Ⓐ Ⓑ Ⓒ Ⓓ   9 Ⓐ Ⓑ Ⓒ Ⓓ   13 Ⓐ Ⓑ Ⓒ Ⓓ
2 Ⓕ Ⓖ Ⓗ Ⓙ   6 Ⓕ Ⓖ Ⓗ Ⓙ   10 Ⓕ Ⓖ Ⓗ Ⓙ   14 Ⓕ Ⓖ Ⓗ Ⓙ
3 Ⓐ Ⓑ Ⓒ Ⓓ   7 Ⓐ Ⓑ Ⓒ Ⓓ   11 Ⓐ Ⓑ Ⓒ Ⓓ   15 Ⓐ Ⓑ Ⓒ Ⓓ
4 Ⓕ Ⓖ Ⓗ Ⓙ   8 Ⓕ Ⓖ Ⓗ Ⓙ   12 Ⓕ Ⓖ Ⓗ Ⓙ   16 Ⓕ Ⓖ Ⓗ Ⓙ

Unit 5: Science, pages 119-122

1 Ⓐ Ⓑ Ⓒ Ⓓ   5 Ⓐ Ⓑ Ⓒ Ⓓ   9 Ⓐ Ⓑ Ⓒ Ⓓ   13 Ⓐ Ⓑ Ⓒ Ⓓ   17 Ⓐ Ⓑ Ⓒ Ⓓ
2 Ⓕ Ⓖ Ⓗ Ⓙ   6 Ⓕ Ⓖ Ⓗ Ⓙ   10 Ⓕ Ⓖ Ⓗ Ⓙ   14 Ⓕ Ⓖ Ⓗ Ⓙ   18 Ⓕ Ⓖ Ⓗ Ⓙ
3 Ⓐ Ⓑ Ⓒ Ⓓ   7 Ⓐ Ⓑ Ⓒ Ⓓ   11 Ⓐ Ⓑ Ⓒ Ⓓ   15 Ⓐ Ⓑ Ⓒ Ⓓ
4 Ⓕ Ⓖ Ⓗ Ⓙ   8 Ⓕ Ⓖ Ⓗ Ⓙ   12 Ⓕ Ⓖ Ⓗ Ⓙ   16 Ⓕ Ⓖ Ⓗ Ⓙ

Reading

Lesson 1   Reading Nonfiction

SAMPLE A

Did you ever hear about the "7–11 rule"? It's about something you use every day. Steps are supposed to have a tread—the part you step on—that is about 11 inches wide. The riser—the distance from one step to another—is supposed to be 7 inches high. Steps that use these dimensions are easiest to climb.

This passage is mostly about

A   the invention of steps.

B   exercising on steps.

C   things you use every day.

D   steps made the right way.

SAMPLE B

Find the word that best completes the sentence.

The ball _____ down the steps.

F   rolled   **H**   rolling

G   roll   **J**   having rolled

Be careful! There are two sets of letters for the answer choices. Skip difficult items and come back to them later. If you aren't sure which answer is correct, take your best guess.

Listening and Looking

It's amazing what you can learn by listening and looking. In this lesson, you will read about two interesting school projects that you might want to try.

GO

Directions: Tomas keeps a journal for his All-Year Project in English. On the entry for this day, he wrote about an assignment one of his teachers had given him. Read the journal entry, then do numbers 1–6.

October 19

"Boy, does this sound like a goofy assignment," I said to Kendra, rolling my eyes. We were walking home after school talking about what Mr. Stewart had given us for homework this week. We were supposed to listen—just listen—for a total of two hours this week. We could do it any time we wanted, in short periods or long, and write down some of the things we heard. We also had to describe where we listened and the time of day.

As we walked by a small corner park, Kendra stopped for a moment and suggested, "Hey, I have an idea. Let's start right here. It's just about two-thirty, my parents won't be home for two more hours, and neither will your mother. We should just sit down in the park and get part of the assignment done. It will be a breeze."

For once, she had something. I told her it was a great idea, then spotted a bench beside the fountain. "Let's get started," I said.

We sat down and pulled out notebooks and pencils. After just a few seconds, Kendra began writing something down. I started right after her, and for the next half hour, we did nothing but sit, listen, and take notes.

GO

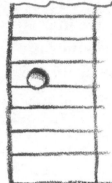

At about three o'clock, Kendra said, "That's enough for me now. Do you want to compare notes? I want to be sure I did this right."

"Sure," I answered. "I can't believe all the things I heard. Maybe this isn't such a goofy assignment after all."

1 **About how long did Tomas and Kendra listen in the park?**

A two hours

B half an hour

C a few seconds

D a few minutes

2 **Kendra said the homework assignment would <u>be a breeze.</u>**
That means the assignment would be

hard.   long.   easy.   outside.
  F   **G**   **H**   **J**

3 **The first sound Kendra probably wrote about is**

A the fountain.   **C** crickets.

B a fire engine.   **D** her watch.

GO

4 **Why did Mr. Stewart probably give the students this assignment?**

F It would be an easy way for them to get a good grade.

G It would give them a chance to work together.

H It would give them more free time for other assignments.

J It would help them understand the world around them better.

5 **Tomas and Kendra live in a city. Which of these sounds are they most likely to hear on the way home?**

A birds chirping

B the wind in the trees

C traffic sounds

D planes landing

6 **What lesson did Tomas probably learn?**

F Some assignments are better than they first seem.

G Kendra is a better student than he first thought.

H Mr. Stewart usually gives easy assignments.

J There is no reason to go right home after school.

GO

Directions: For numbers 7 and 8, find the word that best completes the sentence.

7 **The water _____ in the fountain.**

A splash   **C** splashing

B having splashed   **D** splashed

8 **Kendra _____ a report next weekend.**

F will write

G wrote

H having written

J writing

9 **Find the simple predicate, or action word, of the sentence below.**

<u>Two</u> <u>people</u> <u>listen</u> better <u>than</u> one person.

A   **B**   **C**   **D**

GO

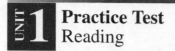
Directions: This set of directions suggests an easy project for a class of students or even a whole school. Read the directions to find out how you can get an "up close and personal" view of birds. Then do numbers 10–21.

Birds: Up Close and Personal

Many schools and communities now have small nature areas. These nature areas have a bird feeder of some kind. If the nature area in your community has a feeder, try this observation activity. If not, try setting one up in your school! The activity works best when a number of students are involved, and it can continue from year to year.

1. Find a spot that is close enough to the feeder to see the birds but not so close that you scare them away. Binoculars will help you get a better look at the birds.

2. Throughout the day, keep a record of the birds that are at the feeder. Note the type of bird and how many there are of each kind. If possible, observe the feeder at the same time each day.

3. Create a "lifetime list" of birds that appear at the feeder. This could be a wall chart with the name of each bird that appears at the feeder. In addition, keep a detailed notebook showing the results of each observation.

This activity can lead to many other projects. For example, you can create a computer database showing the kind and number of birds that come to the feeder throughout the year. It's also possible to do an in-depth study of bird families, or identify times of the day that are best for observing different kinds of birds.

GO

10 **This passage is mostly about**

   F feeding birds.

   G observing birds.

   H building a bird feeder.

   J bird migrations.

11 **In this picture, students
are probably**

   A putting seed in a feeder.

   B taking notes about birds.

   C observing birds.

   D making a lifetime list.

12 **Binoculars are important because they let you**

   F choose the right seed.

   G organize your notes.

   H take good notes.

   J observe birds closely.

13 **It is important to look at the birds at the same time
each day so you can**

   A make comparisons from day to day.

   B get to all your classes on time.

   C meet the same friends each day.

   D talk about birds with your teacher.

GO

14 In the text, a "lifetime list" of birds is a

   F book.   **H** wall chart.

   G computer program.   **J** journal.

15 Find the sentence that best completes this description of a bird.

This bird was about the size of a robin. _____ . I saw it near a pond.

   A My friends and I go there often.

   B Birds seem to be more active in the morning.

   C It was mostly black with red marks on its wings.

   D Robins fly south in the winter.

16 The last sentence in the introduction is about

   F collecting information.

   G drawing conclusions.

   H comparing different birds.

   J sharing information.

17 Find the sentence that is complete and correctly written.

   A To take good notes.

   B Some birds feed early.

   C Using a computer.

   D A detailed wall chart.

GO

18 **Find the word that fits in both sentences.**

What _____ will you be on vacation?
I enjoy eating _____ .

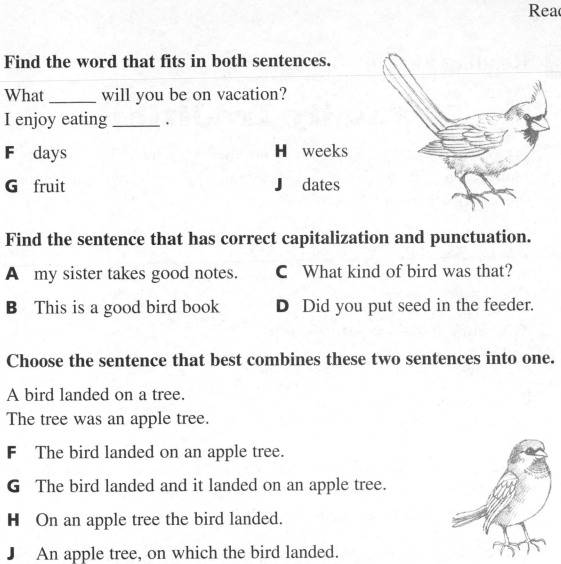

F days

G fruit

H weeks

J dates

19 **Find the sentence that has correct capitalization and punctuation.**

A my sister takes good notes.

B This is a good bird book

C What kind of bird was that?

D Did you put seed in the feeder.

20 **Choose the sentence that best combines these two sentences into one.**

A bird landed on a tree.
The tree was an apple tree.

F The bird landed on an apple tree.

G The bird landed and it landed on an apple tree.

H On an apple tree the bird landed.

J An apple tree, on which the bird landed.

21 **Choose the sentences that best support this topic sentence.**

Birds eat many different things.

A Their colors vary from drab to colorful. Some drab birds have small patches of color.

B Small birds generally eat seeds and insects. Larger birds eat small animals and even fish.

C They also fly in different ways. Gulls soar, but hummingbirds flap their wings often.

D Even in cities, birds can survive. Some hawks now make their homes in skyscrapers.

STOP

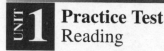
Lesson 2   Reading Fiction

Family Traditions

Many families have traditions that are their very own. Think about your family. You probably have some traditions that are so natural you don't think about them anymore.

SAMPLE C

Buster was the neighborhood cat. His favorite spot was on Mrs. Wilson's car. He sat on the hood while everyone walked by and petted him.

This story suggests that Buster is

A cautious.   **C** friendly.

B large.   **D** curious.

Skim the story then read the questions. Look back at the story to find the answers. Some questions won't be answered directly in the story. Answer the easiest questions first.

Directions: Here is a story about an unusual family tradition. Read the story and then do numbers 22 and 23.

The **Un**-Birthday

In my family we don't celebrate birthdays. At least we don't celebrate them like most families. My friends say I have an "un-birthday."

The tradition started with my grandmother. She and grandfather grew up in Poland. They escaped before World War II and made their way to America. When they got here, they were so grateful that they decided to share what they had with others. On their birthdays, they gave each other just one small gift. Then they each bought a gift for someone who needed it more than they did.

GO

As the years passed and the family grew, the tradition continued. On my last birthday, I got a backpack for school. We had a little party with cake and all of that, and then we headed off to the Lionel School. This is a school for kids who are disabled. Some of the children are in electric wheelchairs, and only a few can walk. I picked this school out because one of my friends has a sister there.

When we walked in with our arms full of gifts, the kids were really excited. Even though we gave them just little things—sticker books, puzzles, that sort of thing—all the presents were wrapped and had bows.

I gave Maggie, my friend's sister, a floppy stuffed animal. Her mom said Maggie's old stuffed animal had just worn out. I helped Maggie open it and made sure it didn't fall out of her wheelchair. Maggie can't talk, but she hugged her stuffed animal and looked at me so I knew she was grateful.

I don't get as much stuff as my friends, but I don't feel bad, even though I want a new skateboard. I have enough stuff, probably too much. Seeing Maggie and the other kids receive their gifts was a lot better than getting a bunch of presents myself.

22 **This passage is mostly about**

A a child's disappointing birthday.

B a school for disabled children.

C a family that lives in Poland.

D an unusual birthday tradition.

23 **What does the family do to show they want the children at the Lionel School to feel important?**

F drive to the school

H have just a small party

G wrap the presents carefully

J give them small gifts

GO

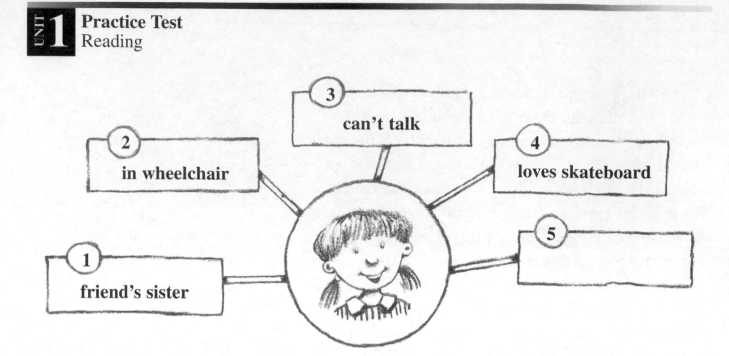

2 in wheelchair

3 can't talk

4 loves skateboard

1 friend's sister

5

Directions: Use this web about the passage to do numbers 24 and 25.

24 **Which phrase would best fit in Box 5?**

 A shows gratitude

 B learns to read

 C drops stuffed animal

 D grew up in Poland

25 **Which box contains information that does not belong in the web?**

 F Box 1

 G Box 2

 H Box 4

 J Box 5

Directions: For numbers 26 and 27, choose the sentence that is written correctly.

26 **A** the party will happen last week.

 B the presents was all wrapped.

 C Maggie will soon learn to read.

 D The kids at the school excited.

27 **F** he doesn't celebrate birthdays.

 G She don't have a party.

 H Got one gift.

 J She hugged her stuffed animal.

STOP

Lesson 3 Review

SAMPLE D

[1]Natural fires are good for forests. [2]Burning dead wood and heavy brush. [3]This helps new trees and grass grow better.

Choose the best way to write Sentence 2.

A Having burned dead wood and heavy brush.

B They burn dead wood and heavy brush.

C Dead wood and heavy brush they burn.

D Dead wood will burn heavy brush.

Directions: Greg is writing a story for the Young Author's column of the school paper. The first draft of the story needs some editing. Here is the first part of the story.

[1]Our town's name is Lost City. [2]It has an unusual history. [3]First of all, it was founded in 1886 by accident. [4]A group of pioneers thought they were headed toward San Francisco. [5]Instead, they ended up hundreds of miles farther up the coast.

28 **Which of these best combines Sentences 1 and 2 into one sentence?**

A Lost City has an unusual history and it is our town.

B An unusual history, our town is Lost City.

C Our town, Lost City, has an unusual history.

D With an unusual history, our town is Lost City.

29 **Which is the best way to write Sentence 4?**

F A group of pioneers toward San Francisco were headed.

G Toward San Francisco a group of pioneers thought they were headed.

H San Francisco, they thought the pioneers were headed.

J Best as it is

GO

Now read the next part of the story.

[1]The founders of Lost City from Baltimore came. [2]They knew about fishing, trapping crabs, and gathering oysters and clams. [3]It was only natural that they would use their skills in the Pacific Ocean. [4]Soon, Lost City was known for its fine seafood. [5]Wagons packed with ice and snow brought fish, oysters, and crabs to inland towns. [6]Seafood restaurants were on almost every corner.

30 **Select the best way to write Sentence 1.**

   A The founders of Lost City came from Baltimore.

   B From Baltimore the founders of Lost City came.

   C Coming from Baltimore were the founders of Lost City.

   D Best as it is

31 **Choose the best way to write Sentence 4.**

   F Lost City was known soon for its fine seafood.

   G For its fine seafood, Lost City was known soon.

   H Lost City, for its fine seafood, was soon known.

   J Best as it is

GO

This is the last part of the story.

> [1]The sleepy little fishing town doubled in size almost overnight. [2]Harriet Johnson decided to build a resort on the cliffs near the beach. [3]With her fortune, she hired hundreds of workers to complete the job. [4]Many of them decided to stay when the job was finished. [5]The workers lived in tents on the beach. [6]These workers the logging industry that exists even today helped build.

32 **Choose the sentence that does not belong in the paragraph.**

A Sentence 2   **C** Sentence 4

B Sentence 3   **D** Sentence 5

33 **Select the best way to write Sentence 6.**

F The workers in the logging industry that exists today helped build.

G These workers, they helped build the logging industry. It exists even today.

H These workers helped build the logging industry that exists even today.

J Best as it is

Greg's friend, Betty, wrote a paragraph about the school play.

34 **Find the sentence that best completes Betty's story.**

The junior high play will take place on Friday and Saturday nights. _____ . The play will be held in the school auditorium.

A Tryouts were last month.   **C** My sister likes plays.

B Tickets cost $2.50 per person.   **D** Did you like it?

STOP

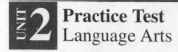
Language Arts

Lesson 1 Vocabulary

Directions: For Sample A and numbers 1 and 2, choose the word that correctly completes both sentences.

Directions: For Sample B and numbers 3 and 4, choose the word that means the **opposite** of the underlined word.

SAMPLE A
The player began to _____ .
Put the new _____ on the car.

A run

B fender

C weaken

D tire

SAMPLE B
<u>recall</u> information

A forget

B remember

C write

D find

1 The sun _____ at 5:45.
A _____ grew beside the steps.

A appeared

B rose

C flower

D set

3 <u>valuable</u> painting

A strange

B expensive

C worthless

D humorous

2 My _____ is in the closet.
Add a new _____ of paint.

F hat

G color

H shirt

J coat

4 left <u>promptly</u>

F late

G recently

H quietly

J slowly

 Try each answer choice in BOTH blanks. Use the meaning of a sentence to find the answer.

 GO

Directions: For number 5, read the sentence with the missing word and the question about that word. Choose the word that best answers the question.

5 Let's _____ the ripe apples. Which word means to gather the ripe apples?

   A eat

   B collect

   C check

   D sell

Directions: For numbers 6 and 7, choose the word that means the same, or about the same, as the underlined word.

6 fast <u>vehicle</u>

   F runner   **H** car

   G animal   **J** computer

7 baggy <u>trousers</u>

   A shirt   **C** clothes

   B pants   **D** coat

Directions: For numbers 8–10, read the paragraph. For each numbered blank, there is a list of words with the same number. Choose the word from each list that best completes the meaning of the paragraph.

     Glass is an amazing substance. Made by heating sand with a few other simple chemicals, glass is both useful and beautiful. In the __(8)__ you drink your juice in a glass. At your school, you may __(9)__ the building through a glass door. The lights inside the school are made of glass, as is the screen of the computer you will use. If you go to gym class, the basketball backboard might even be made of glass. Your family may have pieces of glass as decorations around the house, and if you go to a museum, you might see __(10)__ glass from hundreds of years ago.

8 **F** evening   **H** morning

     G time   **J** mood

9 **A** open   **C** like

     B see   **D** enter

10 **F** new   **H** full

      G antique   **J** broken

STOP

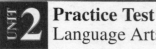
Lesson 2 Language Mechanics

 SAMPLE C **Directions:** Choose the answer that is written correctly and shows the correct capitalization and punctuation.

   A   Rudy gave janet a gift.

   B   We can leave now but, the party isn't until seven.

   C   Do you think she will be surprised?

   D   This cake looks wonderful?

 Be sure you know if you are to look for correct or incorrect capitalization and punctuation.

Directions: For numbers 11 and 12, decide which punctuation mark, if any, is needed in the sentence.

11   **The puppy couldn't find the food dish**

,	.	?	None
A	**B**	**C**	**D**

12   **"This is fun, answered Lettie.**

,	?	"	None
F	**G**	**H**	**J**

Directions: For numbers 13 and 14, choose the answer that is written correctly and shows the correct capitalization and punctuation.

13 **A** The tennis courts are full

     B Venus put our names on the list.

     C Did you remember your racket.

     D This can of tennis balls is new?

14 **F** Tell Mrs Jensen I called.

     G Miss. Richards will be late.

     H Our coach is Mr. Wanamaker

     J Dr. Cullinane was here earlier.

 GO

Directions: For numbers 15–20, look at the underlined part of the sentence. Choose the answer that shows the best capitalization and punctuation for that part.

15 **Winters are warm in Tucson Arizona.**

  A Tucson, arizona

  B Tucson Arizona,

  C Tucson, Arizona.

  D Correct as it is

16 **The play will be held on Wednesday, Thursday, and Friday, nights.**

  F Thursday, and Friday

  G Thursday, and, Friday

  H Thursday and Friday,

  J Correct as it is

(17) January 5 2001,

(18) dear Burt

My mom said you are coming to see us next month.

(19) If the weather is right, we can go skiing, sledding, or ice skating. You can borrow my brother's skis and skates.

See you soon.

(20) Your Cousin,
Sarah

17 **A** January 5, 2001

  B January 5 2001

  C January 5, 2001,

  D Correct as it is

19 **A** skiing sledding or

  B skiing, sledding, or,

  C skiing sledding or,

  D Correct as it is

18 **F** Dear Burt

  G dear burt

  H Dear Burt,

  J Correct as it is

20 **F** Your Cousin

  G Your cousin,

  H your Cousin,

  J Correct as it is

STOP

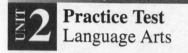
Lesson 3 Spelling

Directions: For Sample D and numbers 21 and 22, choose the word that is spelled correctly and best completes the sentence.

Directions: For Sample E and numbers 23 and 24, read each phrase. Find the underlined word that is <u>not</u> spelled correctly. If all words are spelled correctly, mark "All correct."

SAMPLE D

Harry wrote a _____ to the paper.

 A leter   **C** ledder

 B lettir   **D** letter

SAMPLE E

 A college <u>dormitory</u>

 B <u>assemble</u> a toy

 C <u>loyal</u> dog

 D <u>pause</u> briefly

 E All correct

21 Tomorrow will be _____ .

 A rainee

 B rainie

 C ranie

 D rainy

23 **A** <u>lene</u> meat

 B <u>demonstrate</u> a toy

 C <u>reflect</u> light

 D <u>terrible</u> food

 E All correct

22 Did you finish the _____ yet?

 F lesson

 G leson

 H lessin

 J lessan

24 **F** make me <u>yawn</u>

 G <u>wooden</u> bench

 H <u>accidentally</u> drop it

 J <u>ajust</u> the radio

 K All correct

Don't spend too much time looking at the words. Pretty soon, they all begin to look like they are spelled wrong.

STOP

Lesson 4 Writing

Directions: Read the paragraph about a book one student really liked. Then write one or two sentences to answer each question below.

> I really liked the book *The Wizard of Oz* and think others will like it, too. It was very exciting, especially the part where Dorothy went to the Wicked Witch's castle and made the Witch melt. I also liked the way the characters worked together to solve their problems. Finally when Dorothy says, "There's no place like home," I thought about my home and the many wonderful things I have.

Think of a book you really liked. What is its title?

_____

_____

_____

Why do you think others should read it?

_____

_____

_____

What are some specific parts of the book that you think others would enjoy?

_____

_____

_____

GO

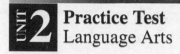
Directions: Read the short story about one child's problem. Then think about a fiction story that you would like to write. Write one or two sentences to answer each question below.

> Shandra kicked a rock. She shook her head. She had missed the bus again, and she knew she'd be late for school.
>
> That night, Shandra set two alarms. She put them on the other side of her room. She asked her friend to call her to make sure she was up.
>
> The next morning Shandra was smiling. For once, she would be on-time with everyone else.

Think about the main character. Who is it? What is he or she like? Why are you writing about this character?

_____

_____

_____

What is the setting of the story?

_____

_____

What kind of problem will the main character have? How will the character solve the problem?

_____

_____

_____

_____

STOP

Lesson 5 Review

Directions: For Sample F and numbers 25 and 26, read the sentences with the missing word and the question about that word. Choose the word that best answers the question.

SAMPLE F

The owner had to _____ the puppy for chewing the shoes.
Which word means to speak harshly to the puppy?

A scold   C alert

B pursue   D inspire

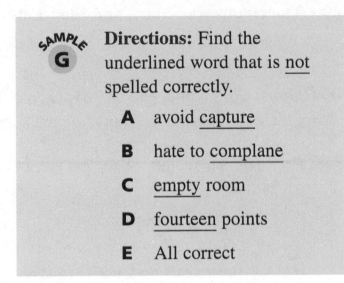

SAMPLE G

Directions: Find the underlined word that is <u>not</u> spelled correctly.

A avoid <u>capture</u>

B hate to <u>complane</u>

C <u>empty</u> room

D <u>fourteen</u> points

E All correct

25 **We hiked to a _____ campsite.**
Which word means the campsite was far away?

A remote   C crowded

B pleasant   D level

26 **The bird _____ from branch to branch.**
Which word means to fly quickly from branch to branch?

F coasted

G hopped

H darted

J paced

Directions: For number 27, choose the word that means the **opposite** of the underlined word.

27 <u>rough</u> board

A large

B heavy

C smooth

D long

Directions: For number 28, choose the word that means the same, or about the same, as the underlined word.

28 attend a <u>conference</u>

F party

G game

H meeting

J race

GO

Directions: For number 29, decide which punctuation mark, if any, is needed in the sentence.

29 **The clouds were dark and the wind was getting stronger.**

!	.	?	None
A	**B**	**C**	**D**

Directions: For numbers 30 and 31, choose the answer that is written correctly and shows the correct capitalization and punctuation.

30 **F** Suzie whispered, "This is a great movie."

G "Don't forget your money said Mother."

H Are there seats up front?" asked Bruce?

J "Let's get popcorn" suggested Wanda.

31 **A** Dad bought seeds plants, and fertilizer.

B The shovel rake and hoe are in the garage.

C We usually camp with Jan, Bob and, Annie.

D The garden had corn, beans, and peas.

Directions: For numbers 32–35, look at the underlined part of the paragraph. Choose the answer that shows the best capitalization and punctuation for that part.

(32) Ricky said, "Watch what I can do." He rode his
(33) bike to the middle of the driveway. And balanced himself
(34) on the back wheel. Il'l bet there isn't another kid in
(35) mayfield who can do that.

32 **F** said, Watch

G said, "watch

H said "Watch

J Correct as it is

33 **A** driveway and

B driveway and,

C driveway And

D Correct as it is

34 **F** Ill bet

G Ill' bet

H I'll bet

J Correct as it is

35 **A** mayfield. Who

B Mayfield who

C mayfield, who

D Correct as it is

GO

Directions: For numbers 36–39, choose the word that is spelled correctly and best completes the sentence.

36 **The _____ is narrow here.**

   F channel

   G channle

   H chanel

   J chanell

37 **Do you like _____ movies?**

   A horrorr

   B horor

   C horror

   D horrer

38 **Three _____ people lived in the city.**

   F milion

   G millun

   H millione

   J million

39 **The train _____ arrived.**

   A finaly

   B finnaly

   C finely

   D finally

Directions: For numbers 40–43, read each phrase. Find the underlined word that is <u>not</u> spelled correctly. If all the underlined words are spelled correctly, mark "All correct."

40 **F** smart <u>dicision</u>

   G <u>favorite</u> teacher

   H <u>gather</u> wood

   J famous <u>legend</u>

   K All correct

41 **A** <u>hardest</u> job

   B <u>invite</u> them

   C this <u>month</u>

   D too much <u>luggage</u>

   E All correct

42 **F** daring <u>rescue</u>

   G <u>solid</u> rock

   H <u>oister</u> shell

   J blue <u>plastic</u>

   K All correct

43 **A** A <u>certain</u> number

   B good <u>citizen</u>

   C <u>ceiling</u> fan

   D <u>Wenesday</u> night

   E All correct

GO

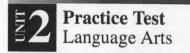
Directions: Read the flyer that two girls designed to advertise their landscaping business. Then think about what you could do around your neighborhood to make money. Write one or two sentences to answer each question below.

Hire us
to take care of your
yard this summer.

We will mow, edge, water, and care for your flowers. Our prices are reasonable. We work hard. We can give you letters from other neighbors who have used our yard services. Call for more information!

Tina and Yani
123-4567

Pick one thing you could do around your neighborhood to make money. Describe what you would do.

_____

_____

_____

Why should your neighbors hire you to do this for them?

_____

_____

_____

How would you convince your neighbors to hire you?

_____

_____

_____

STOP

Mathematics

Lesson 1 Computation

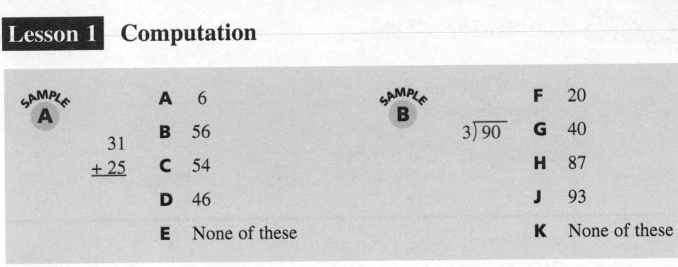

SAMPLE A

31
+ 25

A 6

B 56

C 54

D 46

E None of these

SAMPLE B

3) 90

F 20

G 40

H 87

J 93

K None of these

Look carefully at the operation sign.
Work neatly on scratch paper.

1

78
+ 46

A 32

B 114

C 122

D 124

E None of these

2

0.4
− 0.4

F 0

G 0.8

H 0.04

J 1

K None of these

3

324
× 4

A 328

B 1296

C 320

D 1396

E None of these

4

182 ÷ 5 =

F 36

G 36 R2

H 32

J 30 R2

K None of these

STOP

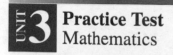

Lesson 2 Mathematics Skills

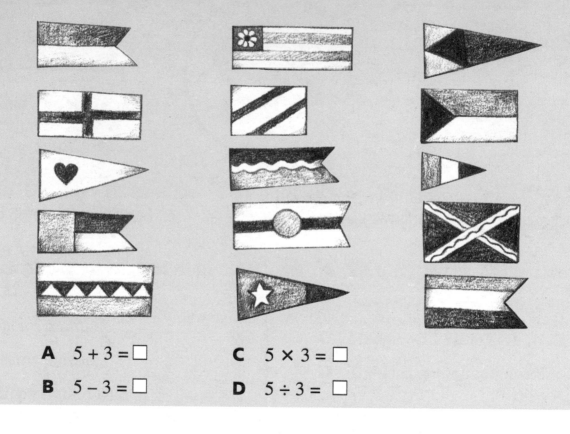

SAMPLE C Which of these number sentences would help you find the total number of flags?

A 5 + 3 = ☐

B 5 − 3 = ☐

C 5 × 3 = ☐

D 5 ÷ 3 = ☐

Read the problem carefully. Look for key words, numbers, and figures.

Think about what you are supposed to do before you start working.

Stay with your first answer. Change it only if you are sure it is wrong and another answer is better.

GO

The Community Pool

Directions: The town of Middlebury opened a community pool with a snack bar last year. Do numbers 5–9 about the pool.

5 The only charge to use the pool is the $3 parking charge. Which of these number sentences should be used to find how much money the parking lot made on a day when 82 cars were parked there?

A $82 + 3 =$

B $82 - 3 =$

C $82 \times 3 =$

D $82 \div 3 =$

6 To be allowed into the deep end of the pool, children must swim 12 laps across the shallow end without stopping. If Jessica has completed 8 laps, how many more laps must she swim to pass the test?

F 3

G 4

H 8

J 12

K None of these

GO

7 Last week, the snack bar sold 1024 hot dogs. This week, it sold 1155 hot dogs. What was the total number of hot dogs served for the two weeks?

A 131

B 1179

C 2079

D 2179

E None of these

8 The 4th grade had their class party at the pool. There are 120 4th graders, but 5 were absent that day. How many students attended the class party?

F 115

G 125

H 24

J 105

K None of these

9 Ms. Fava divided her class of 24 students into groups of 2 students so that each child would have a buddy. How many groups of 2 students were there?

A 2

B 48

C 12

D 22

E None of these

GO

Directions: For numbers 10–12, you do not need to find exact answers. Use estimation to choose the best answer.

10 **Which of these is the best estimate of** $767 \div 7 = \square$ **?**

   F 10

   G 11

   H 100

   J 110

11 **Use estimation to find which problem will have the greatest answer.**

   A 357
      − 63

   C 888
      − 666

   B 615
      − 485

   D 915
      − 769

12 **Leah is making an orange punch recipe in a very large punch bowl. Orange juice comes in different-sized containers. Which sized container should she buy in order to purchase the fewest number of containers?**

   F A one-cup container

   G A one-gallon container

   H A one-pint container

   J A one-quart container

GO

13 Juan kept a log of the number of minutes he spent practicing the trumpet for the past three weeks. Which is the best estimate of the number of minutes he practiced during that time period?

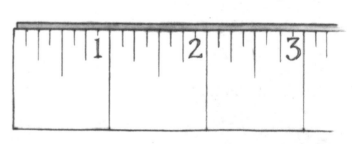

Practice Log

Week 1   128 min.
Week 2   87 min.
Week 3   185 min.
_____
Total _____ min.

A 200

B 300

C 400

D 500

14 Which of these shows the top view of the figure above?

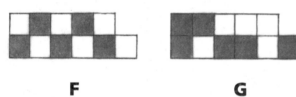

F   G   H   J

15 Use the ruler at the right to help you solve this problem.
Which of these paper clips is approximately 2 inches long?

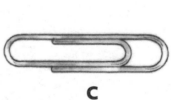

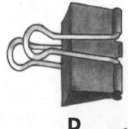

A   B   C   D

STOP

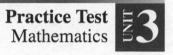
Lesson 3 Review

16

6.89
+3.00

F 3.89

G 3.98

H 0.88

J 9.89

K None of these

17

925
− 6

A 919

B 931

C 4650

D 4660

E None of these

18

5 × 40 =

F 45

G 240

H 450

J 540

K None of these

19

15$\overline{)90}$

A 5 R4

B 6

C 8

D 8 R4

E None of these

20

794
− 318

F 384

G 484

H 476

J 1112

K None of these

21

$\frac{4}{7}$
+$\frac{3}{7}$

A $\frac{1}{7}$

B $\frac{5}{7}$

C $\frac{6}{7}$

D 1

E None of these

22

132
× 4

F 528

G 136

H 478

J 476

K None of these

23

125
− 19

A 144

B 124

C 106

D 116

E None of these

GO

SAMPLE D

150 ☐ 6 =

Look at the problem above. Which of these symbols goes in the box to get the smallest answer?

    A +   **C** ×

    B −   **D** ÷

24 Kim made one straight cut across the trapezoid. Which pair of figures could be the two cut pieces of the trapezoid?

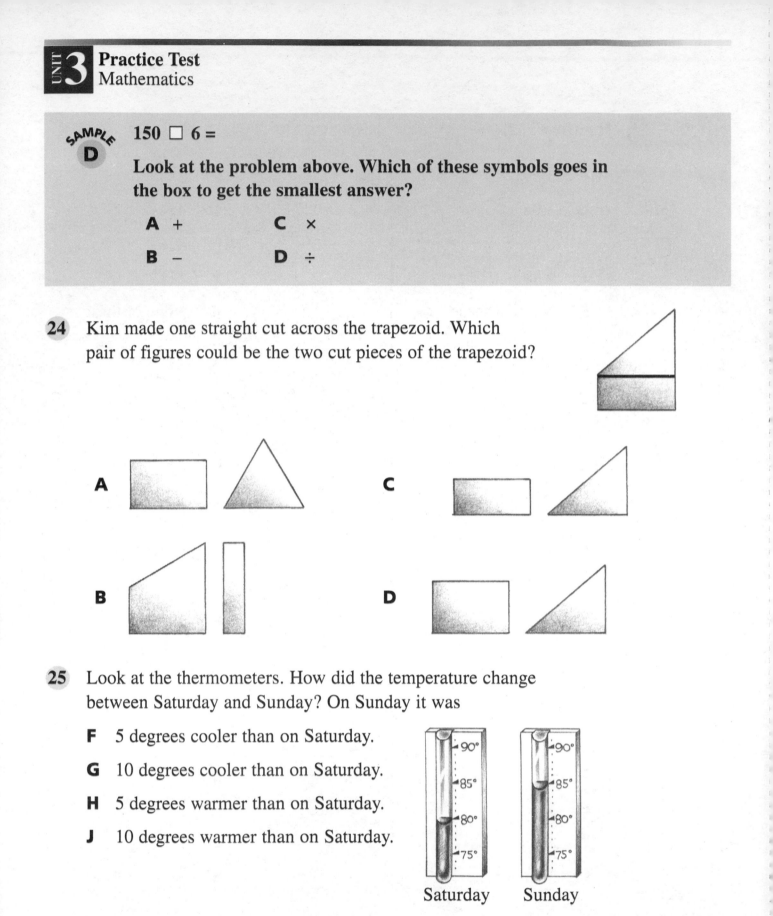

25 Look at the thermometers. How did the temperature change between Saturday and Sunday? On Sunday it was

  F 5 degrees cooler than on Saturday.

  G 10 degrees cooler than on Saturday.

  H 5 degrees warmer than on Saturday.

  J 10 degrees warmer than on Saturday.

Saturday   Sunday

GO

School Olympics

Directions: The fourth grade has School Olympics after the last day of school. Do numbers 26–31.

Make sure you are on number 26 on your answer sheet.

26 **The School Olympics start the Tuesday after school ends. If school ends on Friday, May 30, on what date do the School Olympics begin?**

  A May 31

  B June 1

  C June 2

  D June 3

27 **Yusef is in line to take his turn at the long jump. There are 13 people in line and he is in the middle. What is his place in line?**

  F fifth

  G tenth

  H seventh

  J sixth

28 **There are an even number of events in which students can participate. Which of these could be the number of events?**

23	19	24	31
A	**B**	**C**	**D**

GO

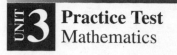

Directions: The graph shows how many students participated in certain events. Study the graph. Then do numbers 29–31.

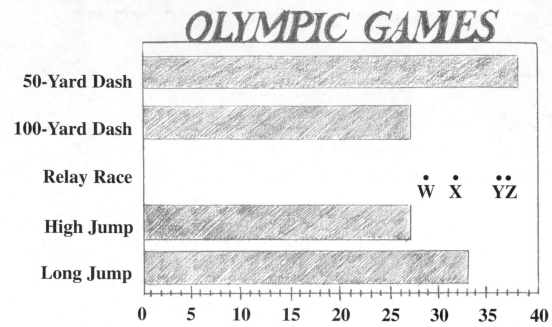

29 In which two events did the same number of students participate?

F 50-yard dash and high jump

G 50-yard dash and long jump

H 100-yard dash and high jump

J long jump and high jump

30 After this graph was made, 4 students switched from the 50-yard dash to the high jump. How many students then competed in the high jump?

A 29

B 30

C 31

D 33

31 The graph is not complete. There are 28 students who competed in the relay race. Which point should the bar be drawn to?

F Point W

G Point X

H Point Y

J Point Z

STOP

Lesson 1

Directions: Study the time line that shows important events in early American history, and then do numbers 1–3.

Important Events in Early American History

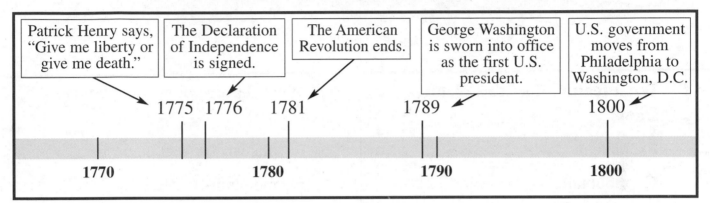

1 **Which event happened first?**

A George Washington was sworn into office.

B The Declaration of Independence was signed.

C The U. S. government moved.

D The American Revolution ended.

2 **Which event did *not* occur during the eighteenth century?**

F signing of the Declaration Independence

G end of American Revolution

H U. S. government move

J Patrick Henry's speech

3 **When did the American Revolution end?**

A during the seventeenth century

B after George Washington became president

C before the Declaration of Independence was signed

D after Patrick Henry's famous speech

GO

Directions: For questions 4–7, choose the best answer.

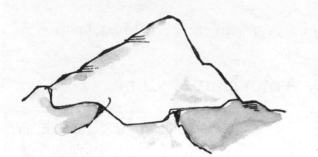

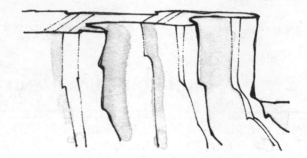

4 **What feature does this picture show?**

F plateau

G mountain

H island

J peninsula

6 **What feature does this picture show?**

F plateau

G mountain

H island

J peninsula

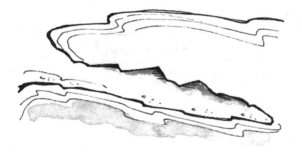

5 **What feature does this picture show?**

A plateau

B mountain

C island

D peninsula

7 **What feature does this picture show?**

A plateau

B mountain

C island

D peninsula

STOP

Lesson 2 Review

Directions: For questions 8 and 9, choose the best answer.

8 Why does the U.S. have three branches of government?

F   voting and taxation

G   transportation and management

H   crime and punishment

J   checks and balances

9 Which is not a branch of the U. S. government?

A   legislative

B   official

C   executive

D   judicial

Directions: For numbers 10–13, find the answer that best completes the sentence.

10 A map scale helps you tell _____

F   distance from one point to another.

G   which crops are grown in each state.

H   state names and capitals.

J   locations of mountains and streams.

11 You use a _____ to tell direction.

A   compass rose

B   key

C   equator

D   line of latitude

12 A _____ map shows an area's capitals, major cities, and state and national boundaries.

F   physical

G   population

H   precipitation

J   political

13 There are _____ continents on Earth.

A   one

B   three

C   seven

D   20

GO

Directions: Read the letter to the editor. It tells how the writer feels about the Titanic explorers. Then do numbers 14–16.

Dear Editor,

   I have been interested in the Titanic for many years and have followed the actions of its undersea explorers. I know that they have been looking for the Titanic for a very long time. It was a very sad day when the ship sank. And today, it is terrible that divers have brought all of the jewelry, dishes, and other items to the surface. I have heard that some items have been sold for large amounts of money. This is wrong. Sometimes, things should be left where they are. Photos should have been taken, but nothing should have been moved. Perhaps future explorers will learn to explore, but to have the respect to leave things as they have found them.

Mitchell Gold
Chicago, IL

14 **The person who wrote this piece is *least likely* to be a**

   F student who has studied oceans.

   G collector who sells old things.

   H person who likes to read about ships.

   J teacher who wants to learn more about history.

15 **The writer's words are *most likely* based on**

   A other letters to the editor.

   B the study of oceanography.

   C the history of underwater exploration.

   D his own opinions.

16 **Where would you expect to find a letter such as this one?**

   F an encyclopedia

   G an old diary

   H a recent newspaper

   J a computer dictionary

STOP

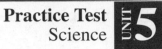

Science

Lesson 1

Directions: Read the table that shows the diameter of each planet, and then do numbers 1–4.

Diameters of the Planets	
Planet	**Diameter**
Mercury	4,880 km
Venus	12,104 km
Earth	12,756 km
Mars	6,794 km
Jupiter	142,984 km
Saturn	120,536 km
Uranus	51,118 km
Neptune	49,532 km
Pluto	2,274 km

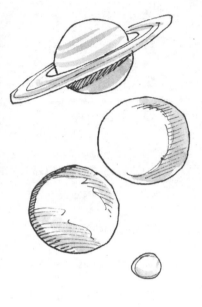

1 Which planet's diameter is greater than 130,000 km?

A Jupiter

B Saturn

C Uranus

D Neptune

2 Which two planets are closest in size?

F Mercury and Venus

G Venus and Earth

H Earth and Mars

J Mercury and Pluto

3 Which planet is smaller than Venus?

A Saturn

B Neptune

C Mercury

D Jupiter

4 About how many times bigger is Jupiter than Pluto?

F 7

G 70

H 60

J 2

GO

Directions: For numbers 5–8, choose the word that best completes each sentence.

5 _____ rocks are formed by heat and pressure inside Earth.

A Igneous

B Sedimentary

C Metamorphic

D Bumpy

6 Fossils are usually found in _____ rocks.

F igneous

G sedimentary

H metamorphic

J striped

7 _____ rocks are formed by volcanic activity.

A Igneous

B Sedimentary

C Metamorphic

D Shiny

8 _____ is the melted rock that comes out of a volcano.

F Marble

G Granite

H Cement

J Lava

9 Ross observes that when he puts a few drops of vinegar on a spoonful of sodium bicarbonate (baking soda), the sodium bicarbonate begins to bubble and foam. Then he puts vinegar on 3 mineral samples. Here are his results:

Sample A: No reaction.

Sample B: No reaction.

Sample C: The surface of the mineral got a little bubbly and foamy.

The best conclusion Ross can make is

A the mineral samples are all the same.

B sample C contains something like sodium bicarbonate.

C samples A and B contain sodium bicarbonate, but sample C does not.

D sample C was dirtier than samples A and B.

STOP

Lesson 2   Review

Directions: For questions 10–15, choose the best answer.

10   **Which item could you pick up with a magnet?**

   F a paper clip

   G a plastic cup

   H a paper bag

   J a toothpick

11   **What are the ends of a magnet called?**

   A boundaries

   B edges

   C poles

   D sockets

12   **In which direction does a magnetic compass always point?**

   F north

   G south

   H east

   J west

13   **Which item does *not* require electricity?**

   A telephone

   B vacuum

   C broom

   D light

14   **What is the path that electricity travels along?**

   F gap

   G circuit

   H wire

   J plug

15   **Which of these would *not* make a good insulator?**

   A an eraser

   B a piece of paper

   C a paper clip

   D a plastic comb

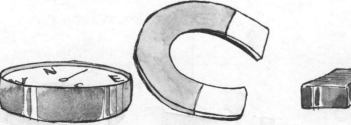

GO

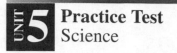

Directions: For two years, Lee and Craig collected water samples from ponds in their area. They kept track of the number of tadpoles in each water sample. Look at the data they collected for the years 1997 and 1998, and then do numbers 16–18.

Tadpole Counts for Local Ponds, 1997 and 1998

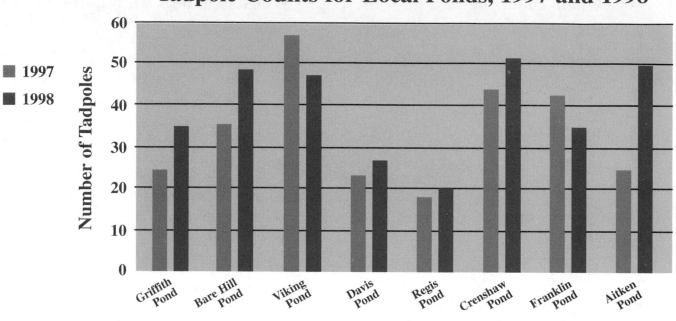

16 **Which two ponds showed a decrease in tadpoles from 1997 to 1998?**

  F Bare Hill Pond and Viking Pond

  G Viking Pond and Crenshaw Pond

  H Crenshaw Pond and Franklin Pond

  J Viking Pond and Franklin Pond

17 **Which is *not* a possible reason for the decrease in tadpoles?**

  A Pollution in the pond made it more difficult for animals to live.

  B Other animals fed on the tadpoles.

  C Lee and Craig did not do an accurate count.

  D More trees have grown nearby.

18 **Which pond showed the greatest increase in tadpoles?**

  F Aitken Pond

  G Griffith Pond

  H Davis Pond

  J Regis Pond

STOP

Final Test Answer Sheet

Fill in **only one** letter for each item. If you change an answer, make sure to erase your first mark completely.

Unit 1: Reading, pages 125-130

A Ⓐ Ⓑ Ⓒ Ⓓ	**8** Ⓕ Ⓖ Ⓗ Ⓙ	**16** Ⓕ Ⓖ Ⓗ Ⓙ	**24** Ⓐ Ⓑ Ⓒ Ⓓ	**32** Ⓐ Ⓑ Ⓒ Ⓓ
1 Ⓐ Ⓑ Ⓒ Ⓓ	**9** Ⓐ Ⓑ Ⓒ Ⓓ	**17** Ⓐ Ⓑ	**25** Ⓕ Ⓖ Ⓗ Ⓙ	**33** Ⓐ Ⓑ Ⓒ Ⓓ
2 Ⓕ Ⓖ Ⓗ Ⓙ	**10** Ⓕ Ⓖ Ⓗ Ⓙ	**18** Ⓐ Ⓑ	**26** Ⓐ Ⓑ	**34** Ⓐ Ⓑ Ⓒ Ⓓ
3 Ⓐ Ⓑ Ⓒ Ⓓ	**11** Ⓐ Ⓑ Ⓒ Ⓓ	**19** Ⓐ Ⓑ	**27** Ⓐ Ⓑ	**35** Ⓐ Ⓑ Ⓒ Ⓓ
4 Ⓕ Ⓖ Ⓗ Ⓙ	**12** Ⓕ Ⓖ Ⓗ Ⓙ	**20** Ⓐ Ⓑ	**28** Ⓐ Ⓑ Ⓒ Ⓓ	**36** Ⓕ Ⓖ Ⓗ Ⓙ
5 Ⓐ Ⓑ Ⓒ Ⓓ	**13** Ⓐ Ⓑ Ⓒ Ⓓ	**21** Ⓐ Ⓑ	**29** Ⓕ Ⓖ Ⓗ Ⓙ	**37** Ⓕ Ⓖ Ⓗ Ⓙ
6 Ⓕ Ⓖ Ⓗ Ⓙ	**14** Ⓕ Ⓖ Ⓗ Ⓙ	**22** Ⓐ Ⓑ Ⓒ Ⓓ	**30** Ⓐ Ⓑ Ⓒ Ⓓ	**38** Ⓕ Ⓖ Ⓗ Ⓙ
7 Ⓐ Ⓑ Ⓒ Ⓓ	**15** Ⓐ Ⓑ Ⓒ Ⓓ	**23** Ⓕ Ⓖ Ⓗ Ⓙ	**31** Ⓕ Ⓖ Ⓗ Ⓙ	**39** Ⓕ Ⓖ Ⓗ Ⓙ

Unit 2: Language Arts, pages 131-139

A Ⓐ Ⓑ Ⓒ Ⓓ	**11** Ⓐ Ⓑ Ⓒ Ⓓ	**22** Ⓕ Ⓖ Ⓗ Ⓙ	**33** Ⓐ Ⓑ Ⓒ Ⓓ	**44** Ⓕ Ⓖ Ⓗ Ⓙ
1 Ⓐ Ⓑ Ⓒ Ⓓ	**12** Ⓕ Ⓖ Ⓗ Ⓙ	**23** Ⓐ Ⓑ Ⓒ Ⓓ	**34** Ⓕ Ⓖ Ⓗ Ⓙ	**45** Ⓐ Ⓑ Ⓒ Ⓓ
2 Ⓕ Ⓖ Ⓗ Ⓙ	**13** Ⓐ Ⓑ Ⓒ Ⓓ	**24** Ⓕ Ⓖ Ⓗ Ⓙ	**35** Ⓐ Ⓑ Ⓒ Ⓓ	**46** Ⓕ Ⓖ Ⓗ Ⓙ
3 Ⓐ Ⓑ Ⓒ Ⓓ	**14** Ⓕ Ⓖ Ⓗ Ⓙ Ⓚ	**25** Ⓐ Ⓑ Ⓒ Ⓓ	**36** Ⓕ Ⓖ Ⓗ Ⓙ	**47** Ⓐ Ⓑ Ⓒ Ⓓ
4 Ⓕ Ⓖ Ⓗ Ⓙ	**15** Ⓐ Ⓑ Ⓒ Ⓓ Ⓔ	**26** Ⓕ Ⓖ Ⓗ Ⓙ	**37** Ⓐ Ⓑ Ⓒ Ⓓ	**48** Ⓕ Ⓖ Ⓗ Ⓙ
5 Ⓐ Ⓑ Ⓒ Ⓓ	**16** Ⓕ Ⓖ Ⓗ Ⓚ	**27** Ⓐ Ⓑ Ⓒ Ⓓ	**38** Ⓕ Ⓖ Ⓗ Ⓙ	**49** Ⓐ Ⓑ Ⓒ Ⓓ
6 Ⓕ Ⓖ Ⓗ Ⓙ	**17** Ⓐ Ⓑ Ⓒ Ⓓ Ⓔ	**28** Ⓕ Ⓖ Ⓗ Ⓙ	**39** Ⓐ Ⓑ Ⓒ Ⓓ	**50** Ⓕ Ⓖ Ⓗ Ⓙ
7 Ⓐ Ⓑ Ⓒ Ⓓ	**18** Ⓕ Ⓖ Ⓗ Ⓙ	**29** Ⓐ Ⓑ Ⓒ Ⓓ	**40** Ⓕ Ⓖ Ⓗ Ⓙ	**51** Ⓐ Ⓑ Ⓒ Ⓓ
8 Ⓕ Ⓖ Ⓗ Ⓙ	**19** Ⓐ Ⓑ Ⓒ Ⓓ Ⓔ	**30** Ⓕ Ⓖ Ⓗ Ⓙ	**41** Ⓐ Ⓑ Ⓒ Ⓓ	
9 Ⓐ Ⓑ Ⓒ Ⓓ	**20** Ⓕ Ⓖ Ⓗ Ⓙ	**31** Ⓐ Ⓑ Ⓒ Ⓓ	**42** Ⓕ Ⓖ Ⓗ Ⓙ	
10 Ⓕ Ⓖ Ⓗ Ⓙ	**21** Ⓐ Ⓑ Ⓒ Ⓓ	**32** Ⓕ Ⓖ Ⓗ Ⓙ	**43** Ⓐ Ⓑ Ⓒ Ⓓ	

Final Test Answer Sheet

Unit 3: Mathematics, pages 140-148

1 (A)(B)(C)(D)(E)	10 (F)(G)(H)(J)	20 (F)(G)(H)(J)	30 (F)(G)(H)(J)	40 (F)(G)(H)(J)
2 (F)(G)(H)(J)(K)	11 (A)(B)(C)(D)	21 (A)(B)(C)(D)	31 (A)(B)(C)(D)	41 (A)(B)(C)(D)
3 (A)(B)(C)(D)(E)	12 (F)(G)(H)(J)	22 (F)(G)(H)(J)	32 (F)(G)(H)(J)	42 (F)(G)(H)(J)
4 (F)(G)(H)(J)(K)	13 (A)(B)(C)(D)	23 (A)(B)(C)(D)	33 (A)(B)(C)(D)	43 (A)(B)(C)(D)
5 (A)(B)(C)(D)(E)	14 (F)(G)(H)(J)	24 (F)(G)(H)(J)	34 (F)(G)(H)(J)	44 (F)(G)(H)(J)
6 (F)(G)(H)(J)(K)	15 (A)(B)(C)(D)	25 (A)(B)(C)(D)	35 (A)(B)(C)(D)	45 (A)(B)(C)(D)
7 (A)(B)(C)(D)(E)	16 (F)(G)(H)(J)	26 (F)(G)(H)(J)	36 (F)(G)(H)(J)	46 (F)(G)(H)(J)
8 (F)(G)(H)(J)(K)	17 (A)(B)(C)(D)	27 (A)(B)(C)(D)	37 (A)(B)(C)(D)	47 (A)(B)(C)(D)
A (A)(B)(C)(D)	18 (F)(G)(H)(J)	28 (F)(G)(H)(J)	38 (F)(G)(H)(J)	48 (F)(G)(H)(J)
9 (A)(B)(C)(D)	19 (A)(B)(C)(D)	29 (A)(B)(C)(D)	39 (A)(B)(C)(D)	

Unit 4: Social Studies, pages 149-150

1 (A)(B)(C)(D)	4 (F)(G)(H)(J)	7 (A)(B)(C)(D)
2 (F)(G)(H)(J)	5 (A)(B)(C)(D)	
3 (A)(B)(C)(D)	6 (F)(G)(H)(J)	

Unit 5: Science, pages 151-152

1 (A)(B)(C)(D)	4 (F)(G)(H)(J)	7 (A)(B)(C)(D)	10 (F)(G)(H)(J)
2 (F)(G)(H)(J)	5 (A)(B)(C)(D)	8 (F)(G)(H)(J)	
3 (A)(B)(C)(D)	6 (F)(G)(H)(J)	9 (A)(B)(C)(D)	

Pages 125–130
Time Limit:
approx. 40 minutes

Reading

Final Test
Reading

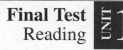

SAMPLE
A

Some people complain when their dog's hair gets all over the house. Others welcome the problem by spinning the hair into yarn and knitting with it. In some cities, you can even find craftspeople who will knit you a sweater from your dog's hair.

This passage is mostly about

A how to clean up dog hair.

B how people love their pets.

C an unusual way to use dog hair.

D why people knit sweaters.

Directions: People are sometimes surprised when they discover talents they never knew they had. Leslie is both a painter and an athlete. Read the story about how she got started painting, then do numbers 1–5.

Accidental Artist

It all started by accident. I was in a summer day camp when I was about ten. I loved sports and was disappointed when it rained. One rainy day my counselor took us to the art room. I grabbed a pencil and some paper and drew a soccer ball. It was kind of fun, so I added some grass around the ball and a pair of shoes. When it was finished, everybody—including me—was amazed at how good it was.

From then on, I still played lots of sports, but I always found time to draw and paint. When I got older and was on the high school soccer and basketball teams, I took my sketch pad with me. In the bus on the way home, I drew things that happened during the games.

When I went to college, everyone was surprised when I chose art as my major. I even got a scholarship, which really helped my parents out. I played soccer, of course, but art was the chief reason I went to college. I knew that when I finished school, I wanted to be an artist.

GO

1 This story is mostly about

   A soccer, basketball, and art.

   B a girl growing up.

   C summer camp and college.

   D how a girl became an artist.

2 At first, Leslie was most interested in

   F camp.   **H** drawing.

   G sports.   **J** studying.

3 How did Leslie feel after she completed her first drawing?

   A amazed

   B amused

   C disappointed

   D relaxed

4 Leslie's scholarship "really helped her parents out." What does this mean?

   F They wanted to be artists.

   G They wanted Leslie to be a soccer player.

   H It saved them money.

   J It surprised them.

5 The story says that Leslie was disappointed at camp when it rained. A word that means the <u>opposite</u> of *disappointed* is

   A saddened.

   B pleased.

   C relieved.

   D entertained.

Directions: Leslie's brother, Lee, wrote this about her. For numbers 6 and 7, find the words that best complete the paragraph.

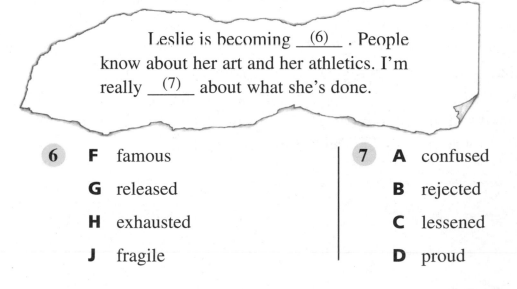

Leslie is becoming __(6)__ . People know about her art and her athletics. I'm really __(7)__ about what she's done.

6   **F** famous

   G released

   H exhausted

   J fragile

7   **A** confused

   B rejected

   C lessened

   D proud

GO

Directions: Read the passage. Then answer questions 8–21.

Snakes

How much do you know about snakes? Read these snake facts and find out.

- A snake skeleton has **numerous** ribs. A large snake may have as many as 400 pairs!
- Most snakes have **poor** eyesight. They **track** other animals by sensing their body heat.
- Snakes can't blink! They sleep with their eyes open.
- Although all snakes have teeth, very few of them—only the **venomous** ones—have fangs.
- Many snakes are very **docile** and unlikely to bite people.
- Pet snakes recognize their owners by smell. They flick their tongues in the air to **detect** smells.
- Snakes have special ways of hearing. Sound vibrations from the earth pass through their bellies to **receptors** in their spines. **Airborne** sounds pass through snakes' lungs to receptors in their skin.

8 **What is this passage mainly about?**

   F keeping snakes as pets

   G snakes' body parts

   H venomous snakes

   J snakes' eyesight

9 **In this passage, *poor* means the opposite of**

   A rich.

   B good.

   C happy.

   D broke.

10 ***Numerous* means about the same as**

   F number.

   G many.

   H few.

   J special.

11 **What does *track* mean as it is used in this passage?**

   A the rails on which a train moves

   B a sport that includes running, jumping, and throwing

   C to follow the footprints of

   D to find and follow

GO

12 **Which word is a synonym for** *venomous*?

F vicious   H sharp

G poisonous   J huge

13 **Which word means the opposite of** *docile*?

A vicious   C shy

B gentle   D active

14 **Which word means the same as** *detect*?

F enjoy   H arrest

G find   J hide

15 **A** *receptor* _____ **something.**

A throws   C takes in

B gives   D sees

16 **Airborne sounds are**

F carried through the air.

G carried through the earth.

H always made by wind.

J louder than other sounds.

Directions: For numbers 17–21, decide whether each statement is true or false.

17 **A large snake may have 800 pairs of ribs.**

A true   B false

18 **Most snakes have very good eyesight.**

A true   B false

19 **Everyone is a little afraid of snakes.**

A true   B false

20 **Only a few kinds of snakes are venomous.**

A true   B false

21 **Snakes detect sound in their spines and skin.**

A true   B false

GO

Directions: Read the following passage. Then answer questions 22–27.

HELPING THE MOUNTAIN GORILLA

Mountain gorillas live in the rainforests in Rwanda, Uganda, and the Democratic Republic of the Congo. These large, beautiful animals are becoming very rare. They have lost much of their **habitat** as people move in and take over gorillas' lands. Although there are strict laws protecting gorillas, **poachers** continue to hunt them.

Scientists observe gorillas to learn about their habits and needs. Then scientists write about their findings in magazines. Concerned readers sometimes contribute money to help safeguard the mountain gorillas.

Many other people are working hard to protect the mountain gorillas. Park rangers patrol the rainforest and arrest poachers. Tourists bring much-needed money into the area, encouraging local residents to protect the gorillas, too.

22 **What is this passage mainly about?**

A mountain gorillas' family relationships

B scientists who study mountain gorillas

C ways that gorillas are threatened and helped

D poachers and wars that threaten gorillas' survival

23 **Which words help you figure out the meaning of *habitat*?**

F "large, beautiful animals"

G "gorillas' lands"

H "the human population"

J "recent civil wars"

24 **In this passage, *poacher* means**

A park ranger.

B mountain gorilla.

C unlawful hunter.

D scientist.

25 **The writer of the passage thinks that tourism**

F is very harmful to mountain gorillas.

G is one cause of civil wars in Africa.

H can be helpful to mountain gorillas.

J is one cause of overpopulation in Africa.

GO

Directions: For numbers 26 and 27, decide whether each statement is true or false.

26 **Mountain gorillas live in African deserts.**

   A true   **B** false

27 **People who live near the mountain gorillas have little need for money.**

   A true   **B** false

Directions: For numbers 28–31, choose the correct answer to each question.

28 **Apple is to <u>orange</u> as <u>lettuce</u> is to _____ .**

   A grapefruit   **C** apple

   B vegetable   **D** spinach

29 **<u>Happy</u> is to <u>sad</u> as <u>beautiful</u> is to _____ .**

   F ugly   **H** pretty

   G unhappy   **J** angry

30 **<u>Car</u> is to <u>driver</u> as <u>train</u> is to _____ .**

   A passenger   **C** conductor

   B headmaster   **D** inspector

31 **<u>Jupiter</u> is to <u>planet</u> as <u>United States</u> is to _____ .**

   F Washington, D. C.

   G state

   H nation

   J North America

Directions: Match words with the same meanings.

32 ruin   **A** annoy

33 aid   **B** attempt

34 try   **C** help

35 irritate   **D** destroy

Directions: Match words with opposite meanings.

36 funny   **F** boring

37 exciting   **G** nice

38 mature   **H** serious

39 mean   **J** childish

STOP

Language Arts

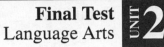
Directions: For Sample A and numbers 1 and 2, read the sentences. Choose the word that correctly completes both sentences.

SAMPLE A

Do you feel _____ ?
We get our water from a _____ .

A well   **B** good   **C** pipe   **D** sick

1 It's not safe to _____ a boat.
This _____ is too heavy to move.

A sink   **C** push

B stone   **D** rock

2 The photography _____ meets today.
The cave man carried a _____ .

F group   **H** spear

G club   **J** class

Directions: For numbers 3 and 4, read the paragraph. For each numbered blank, choose the word that best completes the paragraph.

Roller Blading

In-line skating, also known as rollerblading, might be the fastest growing __(3)__ in America. Each day, millions of people step into their skates and take off for miles of exercise and enjoyment. Typical __(4)__ follow roads, sidewalks, or bikepaths, but "extreme skaters" build half-pipes of plywood or seek expert terrain like steps or steep hills. This sport is relatively new, but it is already enjoyed by people young and old.

3 **A** thing

B people

C town

D sport

4 **F** skaters

G vehicles

H hikers

J results

GO

Directions: For number 5, decide which punctuation mark, if any, is needed in the sentence.

5 "Your brother just called," said Kyle.

.	,	!	None
A	**B**	**C**	**D**

Directions: For numbers 6 and 7, choose the answer that is written correctly and shows the correct capitalization and punctuation.

6
F Mrs. shields writes about sports for our local newspaper.

G Did Dr. Robinson call yet?

H Please give this to miss Young.

J This is Mr McCoy's bicycle.

7
A I cant see the game from here.

B Kim wasn't able to play this week.

C Dont' worry if you forgot.

D The coach would'nt let us in.

Directions: For numbers 8 and 9, look at the underlined part of each sentence. Choose the answer that shows the best capitalization and punctuation for that part.

(8) We moved into our new house on <u>June 5, 2001</u>.

(9) The <u>garage bathroom, and</u> kitchen still weren't finished.

8
F June 5 2001

G June, 5 2001

H june 5 2001

J Correct as it is

9
A garage, bathroom, and

B garage bathroom, and,

C garage, bathroom. And

D Correct as it is

GO

Directions: For numbers 10–13, choose the word that is spelled correctly and best completes the sentence.

10 **This _____ leads to the gym.**

   F stareway

   G stareweigh

   H stairweigh

   J stairway

11 **Hand me the _____ , please.**

   A chalk

   B chaulk

   C chawlk

   D challk

12 **We went on a _____ walk.**

   F nachur

   G nature

   H nayture

   J nachure

13 **Please _____ your work.**

   A revew

   B reeview

   C review

   D revyoo

Directions: For numbers 14–17, read each phrase. Find the underlined word that is <u>not</u> spelled correctly. If all the underlined words are spelled correctly, mark "All correct."

14 **F** <u>shallow</u> water

   G confusing <u>siginal</u>

   H find <u>something</u>

   J <u>sparkle</u> brightly

   K All correct

15 **A** no <u>trouble</u>

   B <u>unusual</u> bird

   C play the <u>violin</u>

   D cat's <u>whisker</u>

   E All correct

16 **F** white <u>geese</u>

   G <u>lively</u> conversation

   H <u>relaxing</u> music

   J local <u>libary</u>

   K All correct

17 **A** good <u>condition</u>

   B book <u>shelvs</u>

   C <u>through</u> the door

   D <u>eagerly</u> waiting

   E All correct

GO

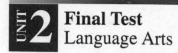

Directions: For numbers 18-25, find the answer that shows the correct capitalization and punctuation.

18 **521 north Main st**

   F 521 North Main st

   G 521 North Main St

   H 521 North Main St.

   J Correct as is

19 **West Hills, PA 11123**

   A West hills, Pa 11123

   B West Hills PA 11123

   C West Hills, pa 11123

   D Correct as is

20 **aug 12 2001**

   F AUG 12, 2001

   G Aug. 12, 2001

   H Aug. 12 2001

   J Correct as is

21 **Mrs Ann c James**

   A Mrs. Ann c. James

   B Mrs. Ann C James

   C Mrs. Ann C. James

   D Correct as is

22 **432 East oak Ave**

   F 432 East Oak Ave

   G 432 East Oak Ave.

   H 432 east Oak Ave.

   J Correct as is

23 **Newton valley oh 42111**

   A Newton Valley, OH 42111

   B Newton Valley OH 42111

   C Newton Valley, oh 42111

   D Correct as is

24 **dear mrs. James**

   F Dear mrs. James,

   G Dear Mrs. James—

   H Dear Mrs. James,

   J Correct as is

25 **thank you for the cool camera**

   A Thank you, for the cool camera

   B thank you for the cool camera.

   C Thank you for the cool camera.

   D Correct as is

GO

Directions: For numbers 26-33, find the sentence that is correctly written.

26
F Those muffins was delicious!

G Those blueberries is so sweet and juicy.

H We done picked them yesterday afternoon.

J Please have another muffin.

27
A We are awful glad you made it.

B We've been waiting anxiously.

C The roads are real bad.

D It's been snowing something heavy for hours.

28
F Ray and I raked the leaves into a huge pile.

G My friend Ann helped him and I.

H Her and I jumped onto the leaf pile

J Ray took a great picture of me and her.

29
A Of all the days for the bus to be late.

B We had to wait in the pouring rain.

C Even though I had an umbrella.

D Absolutely soaked by the time it came.

30
F Last night at 7 o'clock in the school auditorium.

G The third annual school talent show.

H Our class put on the funniest skit of the show.

J Heard my parents laughing and applauding.

31
A I was late because the bus broke down.

B I was late even though the bus broked down.

C I was late the bus broke down.

D I was late because the bus is broke.

32
F Dan ate a sandwich and a apple.

G Jake has a cup of soup and a salad.

H May I please have a extra cookie?

J I'd like an ham and cheese omelet?

33
A Come and see this spider.

B Watched curiously as it spun.

C Here an unsuspecting fly.

D How patiently the spider?

GO

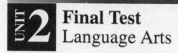
Directions: For numbers 34–43, find the word that completes the sentence and is spelled correctly.

34 That is the _____ story I've ever read.

F funniest   H funnyst

G funnyest   J funnest

35 I grew three _____ this year.

A inchs   C inchys

B inchies   D inches

36 We planted _____ along the fence.

F daisyes   H daisys

G daisies   J daises

37 My brother _____ the coolest gift.

A recieved   C received

B receeved   D receaved

38 I _____ at the store after school.

F stopt   H stoppt

G stoped   J stopped

39 He is my best _____ .

A frind   C friend

B frend   D freind

40 Miss Lambert was _____ about the litter on her lawn.

F fuious   H furius

G furious   J fiurius

41 I can't _____ it!

A belive   C beleive

B believe   D beleve

42 Her cousin is the most _____ person I've ever met.

F polight

G pollite

H pollight

J polite

43 The garage needed a _____ cleaning.

A thoroh

B thurow

C thourough

D thorough

Directions: Find the punctuation mark that is missing from each sentence.

44 Jody please don't forget to feed the cat.

,	!	,	Correct as is
F	**G**	**H**	**J**

45 Max said hed help me rake the leaves.

"	'	,	Correct as is
A	**B**	**C**	**D**

46 "Why aren't you coming with us" asked Julie.

.	,	?	Correct as is
F	**G**	**H**	**J**

47 No, we're not going to the mall today.

'	,	"	Correct as is
A	**B**	**C**	**D**

48 I ate the whole box I had such a stomach ache!

,	!	;	Correct as is
F	**G**	**H**	**J**

Directions: For numbers 49–51, find the answer with the correct capitalization of the underlined words.

49 The last thing I meant to do was <u>annoy the Andersons on arbor day.</u>

A annoy the andersons on arbor day

B Annoy The Andersons on arbor day

C annoy the Andersons on Arbor Day

D Correct as is

50 The neighbors got back from a long trip to the <u>south of china.</u>

F south of China

G South of china

H South Of China

J Correct as is

51 Somehow, the shoe landed on <u>Felipe sanchez's lawn.</u>

A felipe sanchez's lawn

B Felipe Sanchez's lawn

C Felipe Sanchez's Lawn

D Correct as is

STOP

Directions: Read the paragraph that tells about one student's great experience. Then think about all the good experiences you have ever had. Write one or two sentences to answer each question below.

> My violin competition was one of the best experiences I've ever had. I met people from all over the city. I learned to feel comfortable in front of an audience. I felt good about playing for so many people. When everyone clapped, I felt very proud.

Think about all your good experiences. Which one was the best?

_____

_____

_____

Why was this experience so good?

_____

_____

_____

How did the experience make you feel?

_____

_____

_____

GO

Directions: Read the paragraph below about how to plant a seed. Then think of something you know how to do. Write a paragraph that explains how to do it. Use words such as *first*, *next*, *then*, *finally*, *last*.

> I found out how to plant a seed and make it grow. First, I found a spot where the plant would get the right amount of sunshine. Next, I dug a hole, put the seed into the soil, and then covered the seed with soil. Then I watered the seed. After a couple weeks it began to grow into a beautiful plant.

_____

_____

_____

_____

_____

_____

_____

_____

_____

_____

_____

_____

_____

_____

STOP

Mathematics

1

$$
\begin{array}{r}
282 \\
422 \\
+\ 116 \\
\end{array}
$$

- **A** 810
- **B** 710
- **C** 830
- **D** 819
- **E** None of these

2

$0.6 - 0.6 =$

- **F** 0
- **G** 0.8
- **H** 0.04
- **J** 1
- **K** None of these

3

$2 \times 5 \times 9 =$

- **A** 16
- **B** 47
- **C** 19
- **D** 91
- **E** None of these

4

$$
\begin{array}{r}
4\frac{6}{11} \\
+\ 3\frac{2}{11} \\
\end{array}
$$

- **F** 8
- **G** $1\frac{4}{11}$
- **H** $7\frac{8}{11}$
- **J** $1\frac{8}{11}$
- **K** None of these

5

$$
\begin{array}{r}
37 \\
\times\ \ 8 \\
\end{array}
$$

- **A** 296
- **B** 255
- **C** 45
- **D** 166
- **E** None of these

6

$88 \div 8 =$

- **F** 8
- **G** 0
- **H** 1
- **J** 11
- **K** None of these

7

$$
\begin{array}{r}
2.5 \\
-\ 1.5 \\
\end{array}
$$

- **A** 1.5
- **B** 3.0
- **C** 3.5
- **D** 5
- **E** None of these

8

$2\frac{1}{5} + 1\frac{3}{5} =$

- **F** 4
- **G** $1\frac{2}{5}$
- **H** $3\frac{4}{5}$
- **J** $3\frac{2}{5}$
- **K** None of these

GO

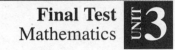
 SAMPLE A Hillary spent between $11 and $12. Which two items did she buy?

A leash and food   C collar and food

B collar and leash   D collar and bowl

COLLECTING BASEBALL CARDS

Directions: The binders below show four students' baseball card collections. Look at the picture. Then do numbers 9 and 10.

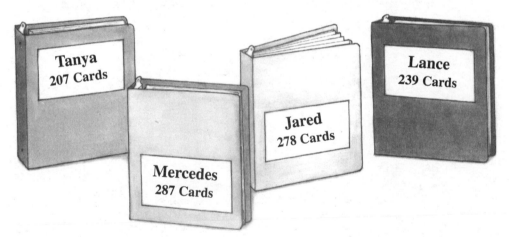

9 The plastic inserts in the binders hold **9** cards each. Which student has a notebook in which every inserted page is full?

A Tanya

B Mercedes

C Jared

D Lance

10 Which of these shows the baseball card collections arranged from fewest cards to most?

F Tanya, Lance, Mercedes, Jared

G Tanya, Lance, Jared, Mercedes

H Lance, Tanya, Mercedes, Jared

J Mercedes, Jared, Lance, Tanya

GO

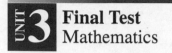
Rainy Day Game

Directions: The picture shows spinners made by four children who used them in a game. Look at the spinners. Then do numbers 11 and 12.

11 **Whose spinner will land on a square more than half the time?**

A Marci's

B Eric's

C Jeffrey's

D Lauren's

12 **Whose spinner has the best chance of landing on a triangle?**

F Marci's

G Eric's

H Jeffrey's

J Lauren's

GO

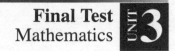

13 Jodi bought cans of tennis balls that cost $2.50 per can. What else do you need to know to find out how much money Jodi spent in all?

   A whether she played singles or doubles

   B how many cans of tennis balls she bought

   C whether she won her tennis match

   D how many cans of tennis balls the store had in stock

14 The computer screen shows some of the top scores earned on a computer game. Ricky earned the top score at level 10. Which was most likely his score?

   F 17,000

   G 18,000

   H 20,000

   J 21,000

TOP SCORES		
Alice	19,000	12
Ricky	_____	10
Walter	17,000	8
Adele	9,000	5
Elena	8,000	4

15 To win at this board game, you need to cover 16 spaces with chips you earn. How many more chips does Marla need to earn so that she can cover $\frac{3}{4}$ of her spaces?

   A 1

   B 2

   C 3

   D 4

GO

16 Lillian rode her bicycle to the supermarket for her mother. Here is the change she was given when she bought one of the items on the table with a five-dollar bill. Which item did she buy?

| F | G | H | J |

 **$3.65** Detergent

F

Cheese **$4.55**

G

IceCream **$3.50**

H

 Coffee **$4.79**

J

17 Yoshi used this clue to find the secret number to open the briefcase. What is the secret number?

A 12

B 10

C 8

D 6

If you double the secret number and then add 4, the answer is 20.

18 Which of these figures is 4/7 shaded?

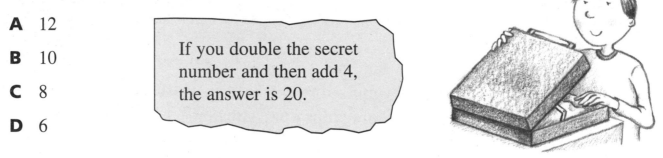

| **F** | **G** | **H** | **J** |

GO

Directions: Choose the answer that correctly solves each problem.

19

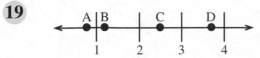

What point represents $\frac{3}{4}$?

A A **B** B **C** C **D** D

20 **What is the next number in this pattern?**

1 2 4 8 16 32 64....

F 80 **G** 81 **H** 84 **J** 128

21 **Which figure is symmetric?**

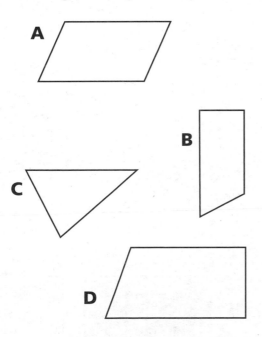

22 **How many sides does a rectangle have?**

F 0 **G** 2 **H** 3 **J** 4

23 **Which unit would be best for measuring the length of a new pencil?**

A feet

B meters

C inches

D liters

CENTER CINEMAS
MOVIE TICKET SALES

MONDAY
TUESDAY
WEDNESDAY
THURSDAY
FRIDAY

KEY: 10 TICKETS =

24 **How many more tickets were sold on Friday than on Tuesday?**

F 45 **G** 55 **H** 75 **J** 295

25 **Which number has an 8 in the thousands place?**

A 81,428

B 78,643

C 42,638

D 29,821

GO

26 What is the perimeter of the rectangle?

F   22 meters

G   18 meters

H   11 meters

J   3 meters

4 meters

7 meters

27 How many sides does a circle have?

A 12 **B** 2 **C** 1 **D** 0

28 What is the temperature on the thermometer?

F   87 °F

G   82 °F

H   80 °F

J   78 °F

29 What is the least favorite pet in Ms. Sheely's class?

A dog

B cat

C gerbil

D fish

DOG	CAT	GERBIL	FISH

30 What fraction does the shaded portion of the picture represent?

F $\frac{1}{4}$

G $\frac{1}{3}$

H $\frac{1}{2}$

J $1\frac{1}{4}$

31 Which letter has a line of symmetry?

A J **B** S **C** M **D** Q

32 What picture shows a fraction equivalent to $\frac{3}{10}$?

F

G

H

J

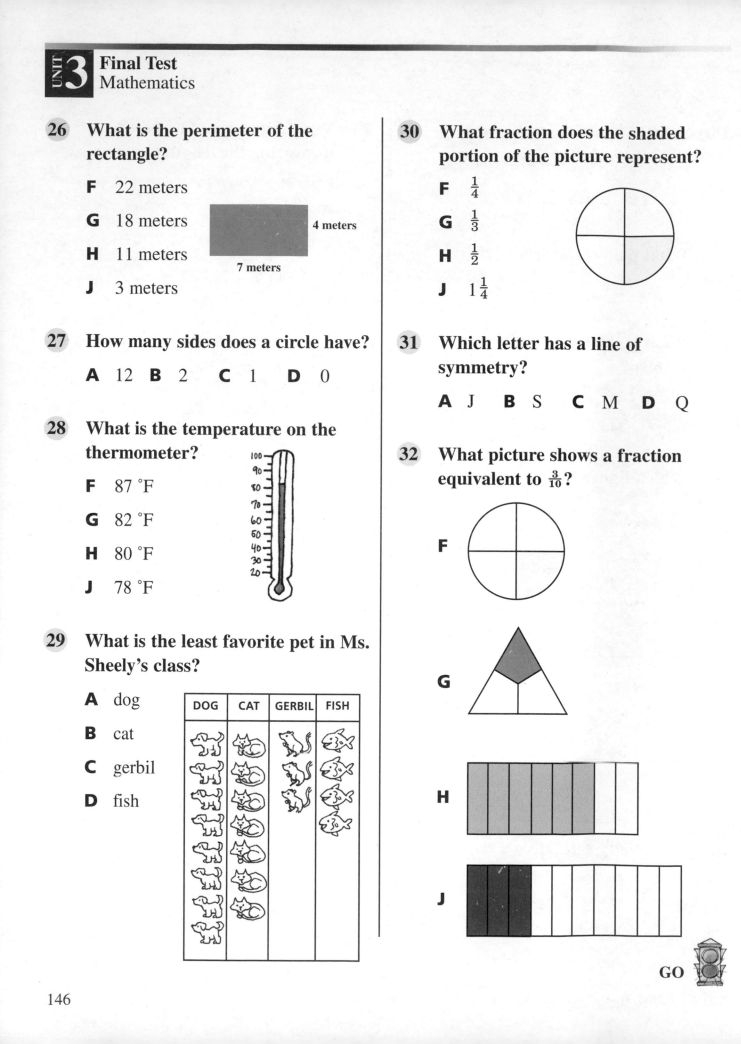

GO

Directions: Choose the answer that correctly solves each problem.

33

$879 + 43 =$

A 1,309
B 922
C 836
D 122

34

$46 \times 82 =$

F 3,772
G 3,672
H 3,662
J 128

35

$281 - 93 =$

A 188
B 212
C 288
D 374

36

$8,941 + 1,278 =$

F 9,119
G 9,219
H 10,119
J 10,219

37

$369 \times 4 =$

A 1,476
B 1,264
C 123
D 92

38

$445 \div 6 =$

F 78 R1
G 63 R4
H 74 R3
J None of these

39

$84.62 \ \square \ 84.26$

A >
B =
C <
D None of these

40

$\frac{1}{4} + \frac{3}{4} =$

F $\frac{2}{4}$
G $\frac{1}{2}$
H 1
J 4

41

$431 + 622 + 58 =$

A 1110
B 1010
C 111
D None of these

42

$12 \times 12 =$

F 240
G 144
H 140
J 24

GO

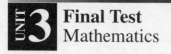

Final Test
Mathematics

Directions: Choose the answer that correctly solves each problem.

43 Colleen found 16 shells on Saturday and 17 shells on Sunday. Al found 12 shells on Saturday and 22 shells on Sunday. Who found the greater number of shells altogether?

A Al

B Colleen

C They each found the same number of shells.

D Not enough information

44 Angela saved her allowance to buy a new pair of sneakers. She had $70.00. After buying the sneakers, how much money did she have left?

F $9.25

G $8.75

H $7.65

J Not enough information

45 David has 72 baseball cards that he is sorting into three equal piles. How many cards arc in each pile?

A 216 cards

B 24 cards

C 20 R4 cards

D 18 cards

46 Toby left his house for school at 7:35 a.m. He arrived to school at 7:50 a.m. How many minutes did it take Toby to get to school?

F 15 minutes

G 20 minutes

H 25 minutes

J 10 minutes

47 Rosendo and his sister combine their money to buy a new game. Rosendo has $7.48 and his sister has $8.31. How much money do they have in all?

A $0.83

B $15.79

C $16.89

D Not enough information

48 What equation would you use to solve the following problem?

Tyrone and Lawrence have a total of 26 CDs. They each have the same number of CDs. How many CDs does Tyrone have?

F 26 x 2 =

G 26 + 2 =

H 26 − 2 =

J 26 ÷ 2 =

STOP

0:10
Pages 149–150
Time Limit:
approx. 10 minutes

Social Studies

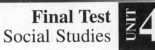

Final Test
Social Studies

UNIT 4

Directions: Choose the answer that best completes each sentence.

1 **The first to sail around the globe was**

   A Ferdinand Magellan.

   B Christopher Columbus.

   C Prince Henry of Portugal.

   D Hernan Cortéz.

2 **The Revolutionary War was fought to**

   F win gold from Spain.

   G gain independence from Great Britain.

   H stop exploration of South America.

   J expand land holdings in Mexico.

3 **Lewis and Clark explored**

   A Oregon Territory.

   B the Louisiana Purchase.

   C the Northwest Territory.

   D Mexico.

4 **One reason immigrants did *not* come to the United States was to**

   F find better jobs.

   G get land.

   H pay higher taxes.

   J have more opportunities.

GO

Directions: Study the map of the world. Then do numbers 5–7.

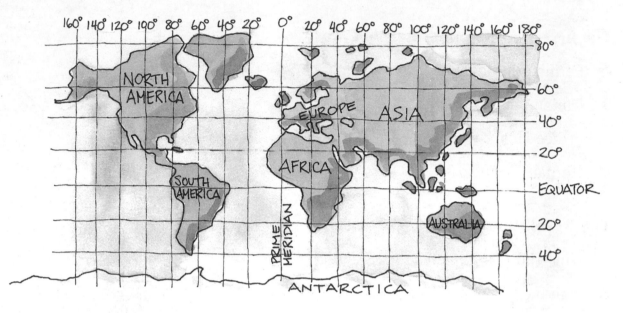

5 **Which continent is nearest the equator?**

A South America   **C** Europe

B North America   **D** Australia

6 **Which word *best* describes the climate in cities located near the equator?**

F cool   **H** warm

G cold   **J** hot

7 **How would you describe the prime meridian in degrees?**

A 120°W longitude

B 60° N latitude

C I40°S latitude

D 0° longitude

STOP

Pages 151–152
Time Limit:
approx. 15 minutes

Science

Final Test
Science **UNIT 5**
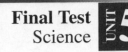

Directions: Choose the best answer.

1 If matter has a fixed volume, but changes its shape to fit its container, it is a

A solid. **C** gas.

B liquid. **D** suspension.

2 How can you change matter from one state to another?

F by changing its container

G by adding or removing heat

H by dividing it in half

J by changing its volume

3 Ice is water in its _____ state.

A solid **C** liquid

B changing **D** gas

4 You fill a balloon with steam and then put it in the refrigerator. What do you predict will happen next?

F The balloon will expand.

G The balloon will contract.

H The balloon will pop.

J The balloon will not change.

Directions: Study Wally's lab notes and then do numbers 5 and 6.

Wally's notes

Properties of Mystery Substance X

Freezing point: 11°C
Boiling point: 89°C

5 At which temperature would Mystery Substance X be a liquid?

A 4°C

B 9°C

C 88°C

D 92°C

6 At which temperature would Mystery Substance X be a gas?

F 4°C

G 100°C

H 88°C

J 92°C

GO

7 Which unit of measure is used to measure volume?

A grams

B pounds

C inches

D milliliters

8 What tool would you use to measure the length of a wire?

F thermometer

G barometer

H graduated cylinder

J ruler

Directions: Read about Jeannie's experiment, and then do numbers 9 and 10.

My Question: Is warm water more dense than cold water?

What I Already Know: If two objects take up the same amount of space, the lighter one will be less dense.

What I Did: I filled a beaker with 100 ml of cold water. Then I filled another beaker with 100 ml of hot water, and I used red food coloring to color it red. I used an eyedropper to put the warm, red water into the beaker of cold water.

What Happened: The drops of red water floated to the top of the beaker. The red water made a layer on top of the layer of cold water in the beaker.

9 Jeannie can conclude from her experiment that

A warm water is more dense than cold water.

B warm water is less dense than cold water.

C warm water and cold water have the same density.

D neither warm nor cold water have any density.

10 What phenomena does this experiment help Jeannie understand?

F why it rains in the summer

G why cold water boils so slowly

H why the top layer of the ocean is warmer than the lower layers

J why it is hard to make sugar dissolve in iced tea

STOP

Grade 4 Answer Key

Page 26
1. B
2. G
3. A
4. H
5. A
6. G

Page 28
1. C
2. J
3. C
4. J
5. A
6. G

Page 30
1. A
2. B
3. B
4. A
5. A
6. B
7. B
8. A
9. B
10. B
11. A
12. B

Page 32
1. D
2. A
3. B
4. C
5. G
6. F
7. J
8. H
9. C
10. A
11. B
12. D
13. H
14. J
15. G
16. F

Page 34
1. A
2. G
3. D
4. H
5. B
6. J

Page 36
1. Answers will vary. Possible response: Insects and spiders both have a head, thorax, and abdomen. Insects have six legs, while spiders have eight legs.
2. Answers will vary.
3. Answers will vary. Possible response: Jack was probably scared when he awoke, but he stopped being scared when he realized that it was his brother outside the tent.
4. Answers will vary. Possible response: Matt probably shouldn't have scared Jack.

Page 38
1. B
2. H
3. C
4. F

Page 41
1. C
2. J
3. A
4. J
5. C
6. H
7. D

Page 42
8. H
9. D
10. F
11. B
12. G
13. C

Page 44
Answers will vary.

Page 46
1. A
2. J

Page 48
1. D
2. F
3. D
4. G

Page 50
1. 159 calories
2. 5/8 of the pie
3. 6 feet
4. 23 cars
5. $15.00
6. $1.79

Page 52
1. A
2. H
3. B
4. J

Grade 4 Answer Key

Grade 4 Answer Key

Page 102
29. D
30. F
31. D
32. J
33. A
34. H
35. B

Page 103
36. F
37. C
38. J
39. D
40. F
41. E
42. H
43. D

Page 105
A. B
B. K
1. D
2. F
3. B
4. G

Page 106
C. C

Page 107
5. C
6. G

Page 108
7. D
8. F
9. C

Page 109
10. J
11. A
12. G

Page 110
13. C
14. G
15. C

Page 111
16. J
17. A
18. K
19. B
20. H
21. D
22. F
23. C

Page 112
D. D
24. C
25. H

Page 113
26. D
27. H
28. C

Page 114
29. H
30. C
31. F

Page 115
1. B
2. H
3. D

Page 116
4. G
5. D
6. F
7. C

Page 117
8. J
9. B
10. F
11. A
12. J
13. C

Page 118
14. G
15. D
16. H

Page 119
1. A
2. G
3. C
4. G

Page 120
5. C
6. G
7. A
8. J
9. B

Page 121
10. F
11. C
12. F
13. C
14. G
15. B

Page 122
16. J
17. D
18. F

Page 125
A. C

Page 126
1. D
2. G
3. A
4. H
5. B
6. F
7. D

Page 127
8. G
9. B
10. G
11. D

Page 128
12. G
13. A
14. G
15. C
16. F
17. B
18. B
19. B
20. A
21. A

Page 129
22. C
23. G
24. C
25. H

Page 130
26. B
27. B
28. D
29. F
30. C
31. H
32. D
33. C
34. B
35. A
36. H
37. F
38. J
39. G

Page 131
A. A
1. D
2. G
3. D
4. F

Page 132
5. D
6. G
7. B
8. J
9. A

Grade 4 Answer Key

Page 133
10. J
11. A
12. G
13. C
14. G
15. E
16. J
17. B

Page 134
18. H
19. D
20. G
21. C
22. G
23. A
24. H
25. C

Page 135
26. J
27. B
28. F
29. B
30. H
31. A
32. G
33. A

Page 136
34. F
35. D
36. G
37. C
38. J
39. C
40. G
41. B
42. J
43. D

Page 137
44. H
45. B
46. H
47. D
48. H
49. C
50. F
51. B

Page 140
1. E
2. F
3. E
4. H
5. A
6. J
7. E
8. H

Page 141
A. D
9. A
10. G

Page 142
11. B
12. J

Page 143
13. B
14. G
15. C

Page 144
16. F
17. C
18. J

Page 145
19. A
20. J
21. A
22. J
23. C
24. G
25. B

Page 146
26. F
27. D
28. G
29. C
30. F
31. C
32. J

Page 147
33. B
34. F
35. A
36. J
37. A
38. J
39. A
40. H
41. D
42. G

Page 148
43. A
44. H
45. B
46. F
47. B
48. J

Page 149
1. A
2. G
3. C
4. H

Page 150
5. A
6. J
7. D

Page 151
1. B
2. G
3. A
4. G
5. C
6. G

Page 152
7. D
8. J
9. B
10. H

Grade 4 Answer Key

Writing

Page 99

Answers will vary, but should identify a book the student has read. Sample answer: *The Lion, the Witch, and the Wardrobe.*

Answers will vary, but should include supporting statements with reference to specific aspects of the book, including characters, setting, and plot. See sample paragraph in writing prompt for examples.

Answers will vary, but should include reference to one specific aspect of the book, rather than reference to the entire book. Sample answer: I think others will especially like the part of the book where the main character spoke out about his feelings.

Page 100

Answers will vary, but should identify a fictional character who could support a story. Students' reasoning should clearly show why the character was chosen. Sample answer: I would write about José, a boy who wants to build a submarine that to explore the deepest depths of the ocean. He will be the main character because he has not been able to follow through with things he has wanted to do in the past. In this story, he will follow through.

Answers will vary, but should include one or more settings. Sample answer: The story will take place now in a small city in California and in the ocean.

Answers will vary, but should include a clear problem and solution. More sophisticated answers might include a character's inner personal conflict, as well as the conflict happening externally within the story. Sample answer: José will need to invent the submarine to help find clues to solve a mystery. He will push past his own lack of ability to finish things he starts as he solves the problem.

Page 104

Answers will vary, but should include chores that could realistically be done by children in a neighborhood. Sample answers: mow lawns, feed pets, clean garages.

Answers will vary, but should give specific reasons that tell why the child would do a good job. Sample answer: My neighbors should hire me to clean garages because I am a hard worker. I like to make things nice and tidy.

Answers will vary, but should show pursuasive techniques. Sample answer: I would tell my neighbors to talk to others to find out how hard I work. I would tell them that I would return their money if they were not happy with my work.

Grade 4 Answer Key

Page 138

Answers will vary, but should include a specific positive experience, rather than a general statement. Sample answer: One of the best experiences I can remember is our vacation to the mountains.

Answers will vary, but should show clear reasons that explain why the experience was a positive one. Sample answer: This was a great experience because I learned how to cook over a campfire and set up a tent.

Answers will vary, but should include specific feelings that make sense in the context of the experience. Sample answer: I felt happy and proud when I learned that I could set up a tent and cook over a campfire with my family.

Page 139

Paragraphs will vary, but should focus on topic and knowledge of an informative how-to paragraph, including time-order words. The steps should be written in a logical order. Topics might include: *how to bathe a pet, how to build a model, how to fix a meal.* See sample paragraph in writing prompt.

NOTES

NOTES